This book is dedicated to all the courageous souls,
human and animal, who have selected to be here to
face the tumultuous journey of learning.

Acknowledgements

No one can build a bridge alone and so it is with writing a book. There were many people who helped me make this book what it is today and I need to thank them.

First, I need to thank Isa and my dear friend, Sheila Trecartin. My musketeers, my personal trinity. Without you both, there would be no book. Our lives merged to bring this message to life in ways that people can never understand. My life is better because of you both and I am eternally grateful and blessed.

I'd like to thank Cate Crow, my editor. You came to me at a time when my self-doubt was highest and I was feeling vulnerable. I will forever be in your debt for your selflessness and kindness.

Thank you to Dr. Steven Farmer for reading my manuscript and endorsing such an important message. As someone who has written about animal spirit guides, your approval means the world to me. I am truly honored.

Thank you to the people who volunteered to read my book. Your critiques helped shape the book into something better.

Thank you to author, Amy Bennett, for assisting me with the book cover, formatting and photography. You took a concept I wanted for the book cover and brought it to life. You are a woman with many talents. I couldn't have done this without you.

Thank you to Peter Wolf for communicating with Isa to assist in the design of his logo. You were so happy to assist, even when I asked for several different versions of the logo to use for the book.

Thank you to author, Val Tobin, for starting me off in the right direction when I had no idea how to self-publish a book.

Last but not least, I want to thank my husband, Norman. You have always been my rock, my teacher. You had faith in me when I didn't. You were forced along this journey with me and you did it with grace, acceptance and trust. You never judged, but took it all in stride with openness and humor. Words cannot convey the depth of my love for you and the depth of my respect.

Table of Contents

Introduction

My name is Isa in this life and I am currently in the body of a dog. However, my soul has been many things and I've had many experiences over many lifetimes.

I have selected this lifetime to move forward as a dog, to be able to understand and experience things from a different viewpoint. A dog experiences life mainly through the basic needs of love, food, shelter, and companionship.

Often a dog's life is quite simple, but I have selected to be a dog who experiences so much more than simply existing in the basic needs. I have brought forward my wisdom from my other lifetimes and my insight is greater, my intuition is stronger. Consequently, I have come to help many people, specifically my human mom who requires much guidance. She needs companionship and love like we all do, but she also needs a deeper understanding of the self. As a result, we contracted to come together to assist one another on this journey in this lifetime, to develop a deeper understanding of ourselves.

My mission is to support her discovery of herself and accumulate knowledge for myself. I am not selfless. I am often self-concerned. But we all work on this and we all work to create a balance in our lives in which we are honoring ourselves and supporting others. In every lifetime we have this opportunity, no matter what journey we have selected.

I began my life with struggle to assist. There are many ways that we can work to help others and sometimes we must sacrifice the self in different aspects to assist others. I have no problem doing that because I know it is important to come from a space of love in helping others. It is important to give to the self and it is important to be open to receive.

Many have gifted to me and I have gifted to many and this process continues as we move forward. I continue to learn, I continue to embrace the understanding of myself and I continue to look to others for assistance in gathering more knowledge because this is truly what life is about.

I ask you to open your mind to the understanding that animals are evolved beings. All animals have souls, all animals have intellect and all animals have intuition, just as all humans do.

I also ask you to open your mind as you move forward through this book to allow yourself to hear the words, the stories, the perceptions of myself and the perceptions of my human mom and others so that this may enlighten you on your path. This is one of my missions, to be able to assist others in their own enlightenment.

If you will honor and be open to the concepts in this book, I can guarantee that your being will reach a deeper understanding of yourself and of the concept of life.

I thank you with love and with gratitude. Enjoy.

~Isa

Part I
Isa & Wanda

Introduction

I am Wanda, Isa's human mother. I have written this book for Isa, at his request. The first two parts of this book are written by me, from my perspective, while the other parts are written by Isa, from his perspective.

I have been recording and transcribing weekly sessions with Isa and my spirit guides for seven years now. This book is an accumulation of those notes. I could not have written this book in this kind of detail, otherwise.

Quotations retrieved from channeling Isa and my guides are left as is without editing. This is their request, which I must honour. It shows that channeled information does not sound the same as human speech and to change their words through editing would 1) no longer make it a quote, and 2) would change the energy of the channeled information, meaning the message would no longer be what had been intended from the Universe.

There are many concepts discussed in this book that may offend people who may not be open to accepting the difference between soul learning and being human. It is not our intention to offend, but to highlight the differences between the human (ie. the ego) and the soul. It's our intention to highlight how human beliefs in the concepts of good and evil create division of mankind.

I would like to leave you with a quote from my guides. Please keep this in mind as you go forward with an open heart.

> This book is a like a buffet for people to select from. It doesn't need to be accepted in its entirety. People need to pick out what resonates with them and leave the rest.

Chapter 1

As Isa's "mom", I give to you the story – more like a process - of how Isa and I came to be together. There were intense events in my life which started long before Isa was even born, and although seemingly unrelated, require history. Some may find it difficult to read, but I write it with gratitude, knowing that from the ashes, came strength and growth.

Isa came to me despite my resistance. The loss of my previous dog, Misha, had been tremendously hard on me and selfishly, I didn't want to expose myself to the pain of losing another dog. I was too vulnerable. It had been two years since Misha's passing and I had just overcome the biggest health challenge of my life.

It happened on the morning of March 18th, 2008 and it was an event I will never forget because I thought I was dying. It started with an enormous banging of my heart against my chest wall and then my heart rate suddenly tripled. I remember getting dizzy and thinking I was going to lose consciousness. I was terrified that I might die because no one was around to help me.

I contacted my husband, a physician, and he took me to the emergency department. I was sent home with a "clean bill of health" only to return two days later. They didn't know what was going on with me, but it had been noted from my visit to the emergency that a shadow had been identified on my lung X-ray so I was sent home with an appointment for a CT scan to rule out lung cancer. My lungs were fine. However, I was no closer to knowing what was wrong with me.

I had been experiencing extreme nausea and thirst. Despite my excessive thirst, I was dehydrated. My skin was grey and my face looked hollow and some days when I woke up I could see that my skin was yellow. I was scared to look in the mirror so I stopped looking.

I could barely eat for six weeks due to extreme nausea. It would also prevent me from sitting up for longer than a few minutes at a time. I would shiver as if I had a fever. I became so weak that I couldn't walk without assistance as it felt like my knees would buckle from beneath me. I developed painful muscle spasms in my lower back and hips, which further compounded my weakness.

I developed painful oily pus-filled boils on my entire back as well as a rash which made it difficult to sleep, or even get a massage for my spasming muscles. I came to view the pustules on my back as a barometer of my health, crying at the sight of each eruption.

I had no idea what was wrong with me. There was talk of my having "mono", but the tests were inconclusive. I eventually called it "the Mystery Illness". After six months, I was in a deep, dark place. I had hit rock bottom with my health for the second time in my young life.

Chapter 2

The first time I hit rock bottom was in 1998, 10 years before the previously mentioned illness. This illness came after many years of chronic stress.

In May 1995, we moved to California in search of warm weather and golf. By the Fall of 1995, while living in California, I had developed tendinitis in my right wrist, an overuse injury from golfing. My husband suggested a cortisone injection in my wrist so I made an appointment with an orthopedic surgeon. By the time I was able to see the specialist, my wrist was beginning to feel better. My gut feeling was telling me not to see the specialist, but I went ahead with it thinking, "What could I lose?" The surgeon suggested a cortisone injection in my wrist to reduce the inflammation but I told him I didn't think it was necessary. Ironically, he said, "Why not? You have nothing to lose." Despite my intuition screaming "no", I allowed someone to override my feelings simply because I felt foolish saying "no" to someone in a position of authority. I wish I could have turned back the hands of time, but in that decision, there were many important lessons I would learn.

I instantly knew something was terribly wrong. I had intense, constant, aching pain shooting down my arm into my wrist. My hand had become severely weak, so weak that I dropped a plate because it was too heavy. My husband said not to worry, to give it a few days to settle down. That day never came. It was getting worse. I had to hold my arm in a sling because my arm was too heavy to hold up on its own. I couldn't sleep at night from the pain and I developed Irritable Bowel Syndrome.

Eventually, I would lose the use of my right hand. It had shrunk in size. I had heightened sensitivity to touch and my hand would profusely sweat, yet be frigid at the same time. I had to walk around in the middle of the desert summer with an oversized golf mitt on my hand, big enough to avoid touching my hand, yet still provide the warmth my hand needed.

My hand turned into a claw from lack of use, as useless as my mother's amputated arm. It wasn't until two years later that a doctor connected these two incidents. As a 12-year-old child, I'd just had a fight with my mother and in my anger, I wished she would die. At the time, my father was building a garage so she went out to the back yard to cut wood. Within minutes of our fight, I heard a funny sound coming from the power saw outside, then the chaos of panic and fear. I looked out the kitchen window to see my mother with blood shooting out of her right arm like a fountain. I knew what had happened. My mother's arm had been amputated. In shock, I ran to every window in our house and screamed at the top of my lungs. Despite my efforts, I couldn't expel the grief and responsibility I felt for the accident. From my 12-year-old perspective, I caused my mother's accident. Apparently, I thought I had the power of God.

I never got over that incident. I became afraid of my feelings, convinced that I had the power to harm people with my thoughts.

In hindsight, I had Post-Traumatic Stress Disorder, but my shame was so great that I didn't discuss my trauma with anyone in my family. My trauma remained bottled up inside me for 20 years like a bomb waiting to detonate.

The physical injury to my hand years later was the emotional trigger that ultimately allowed me to release my trauma.

Luckily for me, I was fortunate enough to have a physiotherapist in California who had diagnosed me with Reflex Sympathetic Dystrophy (RSD), which is condition in which the nerves misfire, causing intense pain.

My physiotherapist treated me to the best of his ability and the RSD was later confirmed when I sought a second opinion from an orthopedic surgeon in Canada. The cortisone injection had caused nerve damage to my wrist, which had led to RSD. As a result, I never received the nerve blocks that would have provided me relief.

I had reached a deep, dark place. Chronic pain does that. The pain was unbearable at times and wore me down physically, mentally, and emotionally. I woke up every morning in hopes that it would all be over, but then the harsh reality would set in. With each passing day, the hole kept getting deeper and deeper. There were times when I thought suicide would be a relief.

I fought back and endured grueling physiotherapy. After 18 months, I finally healed physically, but the emotional scars remained.

My husband didn't enjoy practicing medicine in the U.S., so we returned home to Canada in May 1996. Although we loved the sun and the golf, the move home was welcome. However, within weeks of our return, I developed shingles on my face. By then I was pretty used to pain as I was still in the midst of trying to heal my wrist. If I could handle the pain of RSD, I could pretty much tolerate anything.

By 1998, I was very unwell. I was tired and weak. I had developed allergies to almost everything in the environment. I was getting migraine headaches daily and had chronically unrefreshed sleep. I had become a prisoner in my own home because I had developed powerful reactions to chemicals such as perfumes and cleaning products. I woke up each morning feeling like I'd been run over by a Mack truck. My muscles were constantly spasming and I'd feel hung over for reasons unknown at the time. My brain felt fuzzy and lethargic so it was hard to even think.

I would never blindly trust another person again after the experience with my wrist. Luckily enough, by the late 1990s, the internet had become a great source of information. It was a lifeline for me to research what was happening to me physically. I realized that I needed to empower myself through knowledge. Despite my ill health, I began to research medical conditions and symptoms and tried to learn everything I could about the human body.

There's nothing more empowering than being connected to your own body. This does not require a medical degree, but rather taking responsibility for your own health and never placing that responsibility in someone else's hands. Even when you place your faith in someone else to heal you, there must be a level of participation in which you give consent on some level.

Out of deep pain, this was the lesson I learned from my RSD. An empowered person would never have allowed herself to be injected against her will. It took me many years to understand this wisdom, but we often learn the most from the experiences that cause us so much hardship.

After years of chronic stress and chronic fatigue, I realized that I had finally hit rock bottom. My husband referred me to a friend of his, a physician who specialized in alternative medicine. While noting my medical history, he was the one who connected my childhood trauma to my RSD. He told me that the connection had given him shivers down his body. I remembered feeling confused and somewhat irritated by his statement. "Really, what did emotions and the subconscious mind have to do with an injury?" I thought.

He worked with me to improve my immune system, which meant eating healthy, organic foods. Shortly after my lifestyle change, I decided to come off all the medications that I'd been taking. I hadn't realized that I'd been sensitive to medications, particularly birth control pills, which had been causing my daily migraines.

I worked hard changing my lifestyle and my diet, reading everything I could possibly absorb about nutrition and health. Even though I felt substantially better, it was never quite enough to get me back to a state of optimal health. As I seemed to heal one thing, something else would crop up. Although my health had become a priority for me, it wasn't enough to take me through my second - previously mentioned - health crisis.

Chapter 3

Fast forward to this second health crisis 10 years later, and it felt like every body part was shutting down. I was living a shell of a life, almost like I was preparing to die. "I" was my illness.

Everything in life happens for a reason. An acquaintance named Lori, hearing my story, asked me to come to her office to test my organs via electro-dermal testing, a test which I had used previously to test sensitivity to dental materials. I was so impressed with the dental test results that I knew I could trust the results.

I'll never forget her look of fear when Lori tested me. Every organ, every hormone, every system she tested was in the red zone, meaning my body was under severe stress. She confirmed what I already believed to be true. She told me she believed I was dying, that I would have to choose to live. I was so weak and tired that I didn't know if I had the strength to fight. After all, this was my second time hitting rock bottom. I chose to fight the first time so I knew the kind of strength it took. After contemplating my options, I chose to embrace life. I chose one of the most important life lessons - agreeing to be here.

At the time I didn't know it, but Lori specialized in detoxification therapies. For over a year, I worked with her three days a week detoxifying my body, particularly my liver. In the beginning, it was difficult. Even the gentlest detox therapies made me worse, weakening me to the point of bed rest. But I persevered, and with each baby step, I got stronger.

A year later, I was finally healing and beginning to feel more like myself. The electro-dermal re-testing showed all my systems mostly normal, so this was cause for celebration. Things were returning to normal. Suddenly friends and family started telling me that I needed a dog as it had been two years since my previous dog had passed away. His passing broke my heart so I had no intention of getting another pet. Consequently, this was well-meaning, but unwanted advice, in my opinion. After all, I had just overcome a major health crisis and wanted to spend my summer golfing and being carefree since the previous summer had been spent fighting for my life.

For Christmas 2008, my dear friend, Carol, gave me a magazine called "Dogs in Canada". With a surprising sense of fear, it went unopened into my bookshelf. The heat was turning up on me the more resistant I became. By February, I was hearing messages almost daily that I needed a dog. My sisters-in-law even told me how selfish I was not to open myself to the love of another animal.

Many people judge our choices based on their own needs. This was a great example of how everyone perceives things differently. Although I couldn't see it in the moment, I had never considered this point of view, that I would be denying myself the love of an animal as well as denying love to another animal. From my perception, opening my heart was simply too painful. I couldn't get past the pain to see another point of view. The more I resisted, the harsher the advice. The harsher the advice, the more irritated I became. I wasn't having any of it.

In April 2009, my husband went away on a golfing trip. At the time, I wasn't sure what came over me, but as I was working on my computer, I kept looking up at the "Dogs in Canada" magazine I had shelved last Christmas. I felt an energetic pull to open it. Finally, I did. Puppies were everywhere. My heart opened wide.

My brother, sister and niece had all owned Pomeranians. I was so enamored with them, I always knew that if I ever got another dog – which I wasn't - it would be a Pomeranian. I looked at the breeder ads in the magazine and found a Pomeranian breeder about 90 minutes away from us. In my mind, I still hadn't committed. I thought maybe we could look at the breeder's place to see if it was a clean and reputable place.

I phoned the breeder and she told me she had one "gorgeous" Pomeranian left from her litter, born February 1, 2009. She had decided that he was too small to keep as a show dog. I discounted it because I wasn't looking for a dog. If I was going to get a dog, I would get one in the Fall since she had a litter of white Pomeranians being born in July.

Somehow, I kept moving forward even though I "clearly" wasn't getting a dog. My husband returned from his trip and I asked him since it was Good Friday and he was off, would he like to go check out a breeder, maybe look at a puppy for the Fall? He wasn't exactly sure what a Pomeranian was, but he really wanted another dog. So off we went on Good Friday to look at the breeder's place.

We went to the breeder's and from that moment on, my life would never be the same. She brought out her last puppy of the litter and he came racing up to me, jumped in my arms and stuck his wee tongue up my nose, kissing me all over my face. He was the friendliest dog I had ever laid eyes on and it scared the hell out of me. I didn't want a dog, or so I had convinced myself. I think part of me subconsciously knew what was to come. This was no ordinary puppy and my life would never be ordinary again.

My husband immediately fell in love with this adorable puppy and wanted to purchase him on the spot for my birthday. I made every excuse in the book. I desperately wanted him but I was too scared. Finally, my last excuse was that we were going away on vacation in a week and I didn't know who would look after him. The breeder volunteered to take him while we were away. I had finally run out of excuses and agreed to purchase this adorable puppy. I picked him up on Easter Monday, April 13, 2009 - in hindsight, one of the happiest days of my life and the best birthday present ever.

We had to come up with a name for this little tyke. I was looking on the internet, with no clue what to name him when the name "Isa" stood out for me. My husband agreed that it was a great name. Ironically, it didn't hit us in the moment that the name "Isa" sounded similar to my previous dog, Misha. We made many slip-ups calling Isa, Misha. More on this later, but suffice to say that we did not choose his name.

The first couple of years were full of happy puppy antics, obedience training, and agility training. Everyone he met adored him. He had a way of making everyone feel special, and in a group, he never left anyone out of his affections. He was the most perfect dog I had ever met.

Then everything changed in April 2011, two years later. Isa got sick. It was Easter weekend when Isa started vomiting his food whole, several hours after eating. It was a struggle getting him to eat. It was like having a sick infant because he was only seven pounds and couldn't tell me what was wrong with him. In a short period of time, he had lost 10% of his body weight, which was alarming. He was skin and bones. I had this horrible feeling he wouldn't be with me long.

Around this time, another dear friend of mine, Kathy, recommended that I see an animal communicator. Kathy had been to see this person with her own pets and had found it very beneficial. Both my husband and I thought she was crazy. End of discussion.

Instead, the vet ran every test possible to determine why Isa couldn't keep food down. With each specialist Isa saw, they all remarked how unusual it was to see a dog so young with this condition. After spending $10,000 on vet visits, specialists and tests, the conclusion was that there was no structural cause for Isa's condition, meaning all his parts were working properly. Isa was diagnosed with gastroparesis, a condition in which the stomach can't empty food into the digestive tract properly due to poor movement of the muscles. This causes nausea, vomiting, poor digestion and malabsorption. In Isa's case, they believed that anxiety was the cause. Although not an anxious dog, there was no other explanation.

The vet wanted to put Isa on medication, but I refused when I learned that the side effects could cause kidney cancer. Instead, I took him to a wonderful holistic vet to assist me in supporting Isa's GI tract naturally instead of using medications.

I went through two canine nutritionists without much success. I was pretty much on my own by this time. After much trial and error on my part, preparing all sorts of homemade foods, I'd finally learned that there were very few foods that Isa could tolerate. He couldn't eat fat, dairy, veggies, seeds or fruit. Most meats he couldn't tolerate. As my choices ran out, I even sourced exotic meats like ostrich, wild boar, kangaroo, venison and bison.

My biggest discovery, which finally led Isa down the road to healing, was learning that he couldn't tolerate starch of any kind.

If it was sticky, he couldn't handle it. The only carb he could tolerate was quinoa. I was able to feed Isa a diet of quinoa, turkey breast and tilapia, which he could keep down, but it was very limited.

Isa was finally able to eat without running from his food in pain, but he was still quite unhealthy. Although Isa could keep his food down, he still couldn't break down his food into usable nutrients. His food was passing through his body whole, undigested. He was losing fur from malnutrition and I had become desperate for some answers.

Out of that desperation, I booked an appointment with Sheila Trecartin, the animal communicator who had been recommended by my friend. I didn't believe in such a concept, and frankly, I didn't want to believe, but I had nowhere else to go. At least I was doing something. In a twist of fate, little did I know that my life would take a turn I had never expected.

We've been seeing Sheila weekly since June 2011. This book is written with the assistance of a gifted little dog who chose to sacrifice his health out of love for me. There's no bond closer than a mother and a child, yet I feel that bond with Isa. Some may think it's silly, but I ask you to reserve judgment until the end of this book. This is no ordinary dog.

Part II
Isa & Sheila

Chapter 1
Meeting Sheila

Off we went to our first appointment with Sheila on June 8th, 2011. My husband thought I was crazy and I was a little embarrassed that I had stooped to such desperation. My mission was to trip her up for the fraud that she was. I don't know what I expected, but Sheila would repeat to me what Isa had said to her telepathically. Ah, case closed. Fraud. I mean, seriously? Anybody could make that shit up!

Isa "supposedly" talked a little about his diet, but there was nothing earth-shattering. I guess I expected that if Sheila was that good, all the answers would be revealed in one session, Isa would get better, and life would move on. Just like the magic pill, right? "Maybe I'll give her another chance, just to be sure she's a fraud", I thought, so I booked another appointment.

I saw Sheila the following week, but this was now do-or-die. I was either convinced or I wasn't. I'd been talking to people, asking what they thought about animal communicators and the so-called "expert" consensus was that people can't talk to animals.

Part way through the session, Isa told Sheila that he would like to have puppies. Sheila relayed the message to me and said, "He's neutered, isn't he?" I said, yes. Sheila telepathically told him he couldn't have puppies. In shock, I watched Isa place his head down on his paws and start to cry. The sound of his whimpering was pitiful. It broke my heart.

Sheila looked at me and said, "I think I'm going to cry. He says,

"What is my purpose in life if I can't have puppies? What am I supposed to do?"".

I began to cry. Sheila told him his purpose in life is to make people happy. In that instant, Isa perked up, jumped down to the floor and started to play as if nothing was wrong. I couldn't believe what had just happened in front of my eyes. Nobody could fake that interaction. My head was spinning. In that moment, I knew something had shifted. I had witnessed something very real and authentic. I had witnessed a gifted animal communicator talking with my dog.

I didn't know it at the time, but it was a performance played out by Isa for my benefit to help me believe. His life purpose was never to have puppies. His purpose was far greater than that and to fulfill his purpose, he needed me on board. Mission accomplished.

Chapter 2
The Choice

I think I was a little freaked out by what had transpired because I didn't make an appointment to see Sheila for another month. I realized very quickly that waiting so long wasn't a good idea. I would end up in crisis with Isa as his health would decline, forcing me to go to see Sheila on a weekly basis.

Six weeks after we started seeing Sheila, Isa confessed that he'd become sick to help me heal. Sheila wasn't surprised by this as she'd witnessed it many times. However, my jaw hit the floor. At first I thought he meant to "physically" help me heal and this was safe. However, I was told that he was trying to help me heal my body, mind, emotions and spirit. That wasn't so safe. "What do you mean?" I said, as my voice became more and more shrill. "I'm perfectly fine! There's nothing wrong with me." I did not like the spotlight on me. After all, this was Isa's problem. My denial ran deep.

I was given an ultimatum. Help Isa by helping myself or slowly watch him die because his life purpose was to help me heal. I reluctantly agreed to help myself.

In the next moment, Sheila said, "Great, I'll do a reading from your spirit guides for next week." I stood in a moment of immense confusion. "What do you mean?" I asked. Sheila explained to me that we all have guides who assist us from spirit on our earth journey. "What the hell? I thought you were just an animal communicator?" I said.

I had lived a holistic lifestyle for probably 12 years, but, I'd always avoided the spiritual aspect of holistic health. This was not a comfortable position for me. I didn't believe in God, or so I thought. I cringed at the thought of organized religion, which to me was just another word for controlling the masses through fear. I watched my mother live her life in shame as an ex-communicated Catholic because she dared to leave an alcoholic husband who'd tried to stab her with a knife.

I didn't believe in psychics or spirit mediums, or so I told myself. Truth be told, I was terrified of psychics. I was terrified of the future. I was terrified of myself, for I'd had extra sensory perceptions as a child. At the urging of my "guardian angel", I won a lottery at the age of 17. However, that positive event was overshadowed by the premonition of a friend's death and the intense emotion I would feel at times, but not understand. I had experienced many situations where I got in trouble when I didn't listen to my intuition, yet I didn't see it as a gift. I decided to shut down my intuition. I didn't like it.

In the end, as Sheila told me that she would contact my guides, I realized that I had been tricked by the Universe! I wanted to run out the door and never return. I would have, except for that little 7-pound light of my life. I would do anything for him. I had to heal so that he could heal. That was the deal. If that's what it took, I would do it. From that moment, I made a pact with myself that I would open my mind and accept whatever came without judgement. For Isa. I can't say that I always approached spirituality without judgement, but I certainly did my best. With each little thing I accepted, I would move forward, and that's all I could ask of myself.

Chapter 3
Meeting My Guides

The following week, Sheila brought me a message from my main guide, Aesop. It was four hand-written pages, and the energy coming through was soft and supportive and beautiful. How could I have denied his existence for so long?

I suddenly flashed back to when I was 17 years old, working at a corner store and a customer had asked me to put his tickets in the garbage because they weren't winning tickets. At the end of my shift, as I passed the clipboard hanging on the wall with the winning lottery numbers, I clearly heard a voice in my right ear - my guardian angel - tell me to check the lottery tickets. One of the tickets was worth $100,000, a substantial amount of money at the time. My boss took half of it, but the windfall allowed me the opportunity to be independent and go away to university.

When I think back to that time, it almost felt like the Universe was placing me where I needed to be. I wasn't supposed to live in the city I grew up in, yet I didn't have the financial means to leave. I was supposed to be with my childhood sweetheart, who would be leaving for medical school, never to return.

How could I have stopped believing in this Guide? How could I have been afraid of him? Looking back with my wisdom now, I realize that I attached human emotions to the intuitive events in my life, labeling them as good or bad. How could I perceive that as a bad thing? I think what bothered me at the time wasn't that I had the intuition, but that I wanted life to be easy. I didn't want to be exposed to the hardships, the predators and the pain of life, yet my intuition always showed me that there was always the "light" and by contrast, the shadow. My intuition showed me that we live life in contrast and balance, because without the contrast, we can't appreciate the good. There is always good with the bad; life and death, health and sickness, happiness and sadness. How can we appreciate good health if we've never experienced illness? How can we have compassion for those who are ill if we've never experienced illness?

As I contemplated all those memories, my guide, Aesop, said:

> Please focus now on what you are putting out to the world. Your words and writing hold a vibrational frequency that you are not yet aware of. The difficulty for you will present itself in your belief that you can provide that which you feel will be wanted. Your gifts are many and so please trust, trust, trust and accept that this is meant to be. We wonder often why you do not hold more value to your own thoughts and instincts, for your channel is good.

The last paragraph read:

> Much learning is ahead of you. You are about to embark on an amazing journey of the self. We are here for you. Move forward in confidence and in love for the self.

From start to finish, his message resonated with me. I felt as if I had found my long-lost friend.

A short time after my first reading, I wondered about the significance of the name, Aesop. A quick search revealed that he was an ancient Greek storyteller who wrote Aesop's Fables. I'm not entirely clear about the relationship of my Guide, Aesop, to the Ancient Greek storyteller, however, it had become very clear that writing would be significant within my lifetime.

I looked forward to my messages every week as different guides with different personalities came in and out of my life as needed for my learning. Although the lessons were hard, I knew my guides were always there for me, even though my ego might yell and have a hissy fit at them on occasion.

There were times when my guides would let me spiral, emotionally, hitting bottom, because they knew that's what I needed in the moment. They may have provided plenty of love, but there was no saving or rescuing me. In going to victim, sometimes I would think about quitting. It was too hard. Sometimes I felt like I had a gun pointed to my head because if I were to quit, what would happen to Isa?

Like the Phoenix rising, my guides would leave me to pick myself up from the ashes, dust myself off and figure out how I would move forward. My guides give me the greatest gift of all - the power to choose. They don't want to change me or fix me; it's my choice to change. They don't want to attach conditions to our love; they give love freely, even when I yell and scream at them. They give me the greatest gift of understanding free will, allowing me to empower myself. It's in my own choices that I take full responsibility for my own life. There's no holding anyone else accountable for my life. There's no holding other people responsible for my happiness. It's about choices, learning, growth and self-evolution. This is what we are here to learn.

Chapter 4
The Work

For the first seven months of our work, Isa came to our sessions and provided me with information on his health. Sheila also scanned him energetically each week and relayed to me which body parts she sensed were under strain. Every week he came in consistently with a sore stomach and colon, burning in the throat due to acid, muscle pain, and a sore/itching bum. Other times he'd have fissures, fatigue, ear aches, eye pain, tingling nerve pain up his paws, kidney pain, thyroid swelling, adrenal pain, liver pain or lung pain, just to name some ailments. Sometimes he had allergies, sometimes he had detox reactions. With each stress to his body, my panic would increase, but there was learning in that for me.

Between the scans and Isa's information, it always provided me guidance in setting up a plan to help Isa heal physically. Sometimes I needed to go to the holistic vet for various therapies like acupuncture, lasering or homeopathics to help him through his healing journey.

Isa told me that he's very sensitive to the energies around him. He also told me when my energy was heavy. At times, he disclosed that he felt sensitive to smells and lights too. He often reiterated that he was a healer, that it was his life purpose.

Isa had ups and downs, mainly a reflection of my state of being. I would hit a crisis point and Isa would crash. I would be on an upswing and Isa would start feeling better and note that it was due to my state of mind. Isa repeated to me that he wouldn't get better until I got to the place I needed to be, that he would emulate me physically until then.

Isa told me or my husband not to eat certain foods because we didn't digest them well, or we needed to take specific supplements. But he also had his doggie side. He'd get mad at me - barking at me in that way when he's mad - if I forgot to bring his favorite toy to our session. He'd constantly insist on new toys even though he never played with them, or ask for foods he knew he couldn't tolerate. There were times when he'd get very psychological with food and the idea that he couldn't have treats.

He asked that I not take him on the plane anymore to visit my family because it hurt his sinuses. He'd talk about the staff or the dogs at the play school he attended, telling me how much they loved him. He'd talk about his dislike of cold weather, and insist on wearing bandanas or ties, or dressing up for Halloween, much to my chagrin. How hilarious that my dog was all dressed up as if it was my idea, yet I couldn't tell people that he was the one who liked to dress up.

By the 6-month mark, although Isa was often waylaid by sickness, there was progressively more wisdom to his guidance. He told me that:

> Your opinions aren't accepted so you waste your energy voicing them. You talk beyond people's comprehension so they can't accept your opinions. It's like speaking another language to them, so make sure you speak at their level.

Isa started to make recommendations to me, like practicing a calming bedtime routine to help my chronically poor sleep, or to practice being aware of my thoughts before going to sleep, or paying more attention when I'm driving because I think too much.

This was the song and dance of animal communication. I look back on this time with gratitude for the assistance I was given. Although I dreaded the weekly appointments because I couldn't help feeling responsible for Isa's health, I also looked forward to speaking with Isa each week, in frequent awe of the experience. There aren't many fortunate enough to experience animal communication, and realize how much it humanizes your pet. It's not that I wanted Isa to be human, just humanized in a way that we could speak to each other. It created a connection that we wouldn't have had otherwise.

But this was just the tip of the iceberg. What is clear to me was Isa's patience, quietly biding his time, laying down the bread crumbs for me, before we could get to the next level of communication. Maybe he was too sick at the time, or maybe there was so much I had to learn first, or maybe he wanted to demonstrate the various levels of animal communication, I'm not sure. It wasn't until I reviewed my notes that I realized how slow this process was. I now stand in awe and gratitude.

Chapter 5
A Past Life

It wasn't long - within a few weeks of beginning my own spiritual journey - that I thought I was losing my mind. I was experiencing disturbing flashes of a knife. My husband was away when I began hearing voices in my head saying, "Just stab him [Isa], it'll be easier." I felt a pull that wasn't me. I wasn't sure if I'd become possessed or paranoid schizophrenic. I was so scared of myself that I nearly left the house to stay in a hotel for the night. This happened night after night and it felt like there was no relief in sight for me, nor any forthcoming explanation for what was happening to me. The Universe's lips were sealed.

My guides mentioned that:

> In this current life, in this life as Wanda, you have chosen to heal much residual energy from four past lives. You will be slowly awakened to this. We ask for your patience as we must go slowly. We do this to protect the fragile physical body you exist in now.

Sheila clarified saying, "One purpose for this life is to heal residual energy from these past lives. You're using your life now to overlay it with your past lives."

Sheila said that I would go through a lot in this life to balance out those energies from my past lives. At the time, I had no clue how powerful that statement was.

We decided that I was ready for a Past Life Regression. My first regression was one of three that we did. To me, it was like being under hypnosis, but Sheila was there as a facilitator for the guides, directing me where to go in the regression, filling in the pieces at the end. The first regression was the hardest because I kept tripping over my ego instead of just letting go. I realized that on some level, I didn't want to know what had happened.

Eventually, I saw a vision of a young woman, a knife in her hand, wearing a white robe stained with blood. I had a flash of a child, then a sensation that I'd murdered my child and then killed myself. The woman kept repeating, "I didn't mean to." The emotion that came through me was so raw, so tormented, that I began sobbing during my regression. By the time I was finished, I was completely spent, as if I had experienced this event in real life. For such a logical person, this didn't make a whole lot of sense to me – and yet it did.

Due to the emotion I'd been experiencing during the regression, it was difficult for me to face the details. Sheila sensed that I was either schizophrenic or I'd had postpartum depression, which resulted in me killing my baby, then myself.

The first thing that struck me after the regression was how familiar it felt to what I'd been going through recently. I'd thought I was going crazy, feeling the "pull" to stab Isa, when in fact what I'd been experiencing was the energy of that past life. Perhaps it was in preparation for my regression to make things less shocking for me. The flashes and the voices were from another life time. Once the regression was over, I never felt that pull to stab Isa again.

On one hand, it was a relief to know I hadn't gone insane, yet I was left with tremendous guilt over what I'd done. How could I have done something so barbaric, I wondered? I was prepared to sit in self-blame and self-hatred. But instead, I was asked to view that life from a spiritual perspective, a perspective in which there was no judgment of good or bad, a perspective in which we planned our lessons in spirit before incarnating. I was being asked to understand that the baby had come into that life as part of a contract we'd made in spirit; a pre-birth planning.

It took a lot of processing but I was finally able to adopt that perspective. It's such an odd way of viewing life, especially when society is conditioned by religion to view people as good or evil. But what if we come to this life from the dark to learn as well as provide learning for others? Sometimes we come from the light and sometimes we come from the dark. What's important is the learning. What a beautiful way to look at life. The downfall of organized religion, from my perspective, is that it can't fully explain the "unfairness" of life such as pain, death and murder yet still stand from a place of love. Therefore, any religion that views us as "sinners" separates us from the source of love; but the goal of life is love. The goal is reaching unity with all that is through love.

Timing is a funny thing. As my logical mind looks back on events, I wonder why I didn't connect the dots sooner. It would take me three months to wonder if that murdered baby in my past life was connected to someone in this life. My guides wouldn't give me the answer, but they said it would come. It took two weeks to arrive.

I was driving Isa home from doggie play school when I suddenly had this intense tingling all over my body and an all-knowing realization that Isa had been my murdered baby. I energetically and mentally watched all the pieces fall into place - the flashes of the knife, the voice telling me to stab Isa. I was getting flashes of that past life and I knew with 100% certainty that Isa was that baby I had murdered.

Overcome with emotion, I began sobbing in the car. Clearly, I hadn't fully processed the concepts of pre-birth planning. As I drove home, I kept saying to Isa between sobs, "I'm so sorry, I'm so sorry." When I parked in the driveway, I picked him up from the backseat of the car and hugged him tightly as if he were my child.

What strikes me in hindsight is the realness of these events and how raw the emotions were inside me. I don't typically sob unless I'm feeling immense grief, but that grief was intense and raw. Logically, I can only say that what my guides had said was true. I was healing residual energy from that past life.

Now I understood the pressure for me to get a dog. It hadn't been about getting any dog. It was about getting Isa. He was waiting for me to pick him up.

I discussed what had happened during our next session. I learned that Isa had been a human soul in previous lives and was part of my soul group. Although this was rare, Sheila knew of a few animals having incarnated after being human. Isa came to me in the body of a dog because it had been my choice in spirit to balance karma - for the murder of my child – by living this life without children.

I had spent much of my fertile years ill and never felt the desire to have children. A part of me knew that I didn't have the energy required to be a parent. It wasn't that I disliked children; I'd had a job as an abuse investigator dedicated to protecting them. But a part of me knew I shouldn't have them. At the time, I didn't understand the feeling, but I do now. My life wasn't about coming here to have a child; it was about coming here not to have a child. Isa entering my life as a dog was the only acceptable way for me.

Isa explained to us that he wouldn't be with me for a long time like a child would, so the time I needed to learn these lessons was short. He said, "You'll learn and you'll get it and it will be fine. Then I'll go to spirit and we'll meet up there and discuss things."

Isa added that he'd taken on the same issues as me so that I would recognize them in myself. He was trying to help me heal, even back then as my baby. That's why he came to me, to help heal my heart. He said, "I get adamant with you whenever you don't learn or listen because I realize it's so important. We only have one shot at this so I'm always trying to tell you, trying to show you, what you need to do."

Sheila remarked that this was why Isa was different from most dogs. He'd worked so hard to get to me. He was trying to play it exactly right so that I'd find him and take him home.

I stand in awe when I think about all the events that I thought were random; my friends constantly telling me that I needed a dog, a girlfriend giving me a "Dogs in Canada" magazine which would locate Isa's breeder for me, the breeder telling me that she had intended to keep Isa for a show dog, but had just decided to give him up because she didn't think he would grow large enough. Ironically, weeks after I got him, he had a growth spurt.

Synchronicity was at play. Synchronicity means that events are not random, but meaningful coincidences. How often do we dismiss coincidences in our lives and pass it off as random? How often do we miss out on opportunities because we don't see the connections between events, too absorbed in negative mind-thoughts, worry and fear? Synchronicity would play a large part in my life moving forward as I learned the art of universal communication.

Chapter 6
Things are Never as They Seem

Up until this point, most of my interactions and communications with Isa had been focused on his health. It was now seven months since our work had begun and this was the first time that Isa had clearly shown me - in a way I understood - that he was communicating at a level higher than canine. He was speaking to me from a spiritual/soul level, providing spiritual as well as psychic messages. Often, he told me that the energy of various animals were working with me as spiritual messengers to assist me on my journey and that I should research their messages. Over the years, this helped me learn a great deal about the messages that animals bring to each of us.

There was often a dance where Isa and my guides worked together to bring me my current lessons. Just when I thought I'd seen it all, I realized yet again that Isa was more than what he appeared to be.

I mentioned earlier that I didn't choose Isa's name. Several people asked me what his name meant, since it wasn't very common. Finally, one day, after numerous questions, I went online to find the origins of Isa's name. Imagine my surprise when I learned that the male version of the name is Arabic for Jesus. In the Islamic religion, Jesus was a prophet, a messenger of God. I felt a wave of shivers as I connected that Isa's role in this life was to be a spiritual messenger. I had asked Isa if he'd chosen his name and he confirmed that he'd planted the name in my mind, that he wanted me to figure out the connections.

I no longer looked at Isa as a dog. Of course, I saw him as a dog, but now I also felt his soul, and it touched me and others in the most profound of ways. I couldn't believe how often people referred to him as human-like or nickname him "little man".

What an important lesson. It's a mission that Isa had been compelled to pursue in his life. Never judge animals as being inferior. When it comes down to it, we are all souls with different paths. Who are we to judge one soul as more superior than another?

Chapter 7
A Lesson in Fear

Since revealing his special gifts, Isa's first big spiritual message to me was that I needed to watch my dreams. He said I'm being challenged in my dreams, and the purpose of being challenged is to face things I don't want to see.

Of course, this triggered my fear of dreams, since I'd once predicted a friend's death in my dream. I feared that every time I dreamed, something bad would happen.

As a child, I'd experienced a lot of nightmares, as well as night terrors, from which I'd had difficulty emerging. I often sleep walked, sometimes waking up outside in the middle of the night.

As an adult, I'd experienced terrifying instances of what some might call sleep paralysis, something I still don't fully understand to this day. Coming out of sleep, my mind was awake but my body was still paralyzed. I'd sense negative energy, and it felt as if I was being pinned down by a force greater than myself. One time I felt like my body wasn't on the bed, like I was levitating. I was panicking but could do nothing about it. Was it a negative entity in the room or was I experiencing a hallucination during a waking state? I don't know, but it terrified me. With each instance of sleep paralysis, I was unable to sleep in that room again because of the experience.

In hindsight, I never understood the magnitude of fear connected to my sleep. No wonder I've struggled my entire life with the inability to maintain a deep level of sleep.

From a sleep study done in 2008, I was diagnosed with alpha wave intrusion, a situation in which the brain constantly gets interrupted by lighter "waking state" brain waves during deep levels of sleep. This results in very shallow sleep. We often take physical symptoms at face value, never delving into the true cause of physical ailments, which often have an emotional component at their roots. Was this not a subconscious protective mechanism?

When I think about it, it seemed beautifully orchestrated. My subconscious mind was protecting me, constantly yanking me out of deep sleep so I wouldn't have to dream, so I wouldn't have to face the fears I needed to face. But it all backfired. This protective mechanism was directly related to my chronic fibromyalgia and poor health, since the body needs deep levels of sleep for daily repair.

Now here I was in my session with Isa warning me that I'm being challenged in my sleep. I remember feeling physically sick at the prospect of facing my dreams and said I didn't want to face them.

Sheila had to help me with my resistance. She said:

> He's saying it's a key to help you know what to get rid
> of. You didn't want to feel when I first met you either
> and he brought you through. Now look at how wonder-
> fully you're doing. So we have to trust him. He knows
> quite a bit so he's saying, your dreams are not harming
> you, they're just getting you to pay attention to what's
> still there that you need to clear.

I began crying. This was a core fear I did not want to face. Sheila continued further, saying:

It's a gauge to say ok, this is what we're to clear next so if it's fear, fear of predictions or psychic ability, he's just saying you're going to be challenged by that because you're not comfortable with it. But if you pay attention to your dreams and you tell me, then we can clear it.

As I put this to words, I'm realizing I didn't fully clear this fear. It was such an entrenched fear for me, but I think it moved me along the path of facing my fears, which were many. I think back on my life and the intensity of the fears I had to navigate, and I understand why I was tired and sick all the time.

Sheila summarized it well during our session when she said that, "Fear is an obstacle that prevents you from moving forward."

As I contemplate those words, I realize that my fear of sleeping seriously held me back, and I can't help but feel the sense that my understanding of this sleep issue is only the tip of the iceberg, that I will be facing the darkness that lurks beneath.

But timing is everything. I may not have been ready to face those fears in the beginning, but in time, I was.

Chapter 8
A Lesson in Belief

One day, Isa gave me some tough love. He told me that:

> It's about time you smarten up and take control, and realize that you have more power than you allow yourself to believe. Stop allowing things to happen to you.
>
> You're allowing things to bother you too much and that's a choice you're making and it's affecting me. I'm just going to keep getting worse until you stop, until you choose to stop because you don't listen any other way. It's just a matter of changing your behavior and changing your thoughts.

Ouch!! It seemed so simple, yet it wasn't. I wanted to just take a pretty pink pill of "changing behavior" and a blue pill of "chang--ing thoughts" and be done with it. Sigh. But who ever said this would be easy? Almost as sure as death and taxes, I could always count on Isa to up the ante for me.

I knew exactly what he was talking about. I thought I'd been do-ing well but then something I didn't understand happened to me. A few nights earlier, I had gone to bed and, as usual, energeti-cally protected myself before sleeping. However, I found myself in a very real dream, feeling a sucking sensation like something being torn out from beneath my chest. I had the instinct to hold onto my chest to hold whatever was pulling inside me, like something was trying to steal my heart.

I woke up with my hand covering my heart, and I felt a throbbing. This was strange. Now I could feel negative energy and visions swirling around in my mind. When I opened my eyes in the dark, the same swirling was there. When I asked my guides if I was being psychically attacked, my body started to shiver all over. Confirmation.

Before finishing with this story, I need to back up a week. As you've probably come to learn by now, everything is connected. The week before, I'd shifted from a conscious state to a sleeping state too quickly - so I'd later learned - and I'd felt myself being sucked downwards into a vacuum. It frightened me because I didn't know what it was so, in fear, I'd resisted whatever was happening. Despite my resistance, I had no control, fear being my last thought before going deep into unconsciousness.

For clarity, I discussed it with Sheila and my guides during our session. It had reminded me of those other times in my life when I'd been paralyzed when waking up, so I'd asked my guides what had happened during those times. Their explanation, as opposed to the scientific explanation of sleep paralysis, was that:

> It was a spirit battling you. The negative spirit can come and steal from you, steal your energy. It makes them more powerful if they can suck energy from you or they can step into your body and try to take over and channel through you.
>
> What the negative spirit does is feeds on fear so it makes people prey [for the spirit] because whoever is standing in fear is vulnerable, which makes them weak.

Sheila told me to, "Ask for protection, trust, be more positive and don't tolerate it. Tell the spirit to go, that it's not welcome and it has to leave."

This was a lesson in intention, an action or plan that we create in the mind. Whatever you hold in your thoughts is what you bring to your world.

Sheila explained further that:

> Intention is definitely the secret of life so whatever intention you hold, that's what is going to be achieved. If you're sending out that you're vulnerable and afraid of spirits, then it will come to you.
>
> It's Native tradition that every time we evolve spiritually, negative spirits will come to test us. Negative spirits come to challenge our belief in ourselves to see if we're worthy to go to the next level. It's not necessarily a bad thing. It helps us to understand whether we're ready. It shows us where we are, whether we want to stay stuck, or whether we can progress forward through the fear.
>
> Spiritually, you're progressing really quickly so I wouldn't be surprised if you're faced with that quite frequently. Just protect yourself and protect your house. Mostly they'll come in your dream state because you're more vulnerable. If you find your hands, you have control of your dream so if anything does come and it's negative, consciously find your hands and you'll have full power.

I love how the universe prepares me for my lessons. One benign event like falling asleep too quickly triggered a discussion about sleep and being challenged in my sleep. The next thing I knew, I was being tested to see if I'd learned the course material.

Now, to continue the story, I'd just received confirmation from my guides that I was being challenged. I was relieved that we'd prepared for this lesson because I remembered them telling me not to go to fear. I was able to stand back from the fear and calm myself. I called in my guides for protection and with each moment of experiencing peace and calm, it all went away.

Since I was still a bit freaked out, I can't say I passed with flying colors. I didn't sleep well and I was nervous. This was one reason that Isa had been so frustrated with me. He told me he'd keep getting worse until I started to change my behavior and my thoughts. Sheila was also right when she said I'd be challenged often.

Three months prior to this event, Isa had told me that I needed to watch the movie Beetlejuice to understand the concept of how to deal with negative spirits. Beetlejuice was supposed to be an evil spirit but they made him out to be comical and harmless in a detached way. If I could view negative spirit that way, it would give me more power.

He was right. And this was a lesson I had to learn and would continue to learn. Three years later, we had a negative spirit visit the bedroom for a few months. I wouldn't call it an evil spirit, just a spirit who liked to try to scare me. I wouldn't have known of its existence except for the fact that Isa would get extremely anxious in the bedroom. He wanted out.

This spirit had entered my dreams a couple of times, trying to scare me. One morning, I woke up from a dream where this spirit had been trying to scare me and when I scratched the top of my ear, it was not my hand. It felt like an old man's leathery, wrinkled, gnarly hand. The fingers were big, and didn't fit into the fold of my ear. I felt that tingling of confirmation when I asked my guides if it was the spirit's hand. I asked for protection and consciously focused on going to peace.

Things were okay until my husband went away on a trip and this spirit decided to torment me. I'd never heard it before, but the first night on my own in our empty house, I heard it whisper in my right ear, "We're going to have fun tonight." It started saying horrible things to scare me. Instead of shutting the channel down, I listened. Since Isa's sensitive to energies, he got freaked out when he became aware of its presence. But because this was my lesson, he couldn't interfere and remove the spirit. I fed off Isa's anxiety and ended up sleeping downstairs in my office with the lights on. The whole time, I could sense this spirit's excitement in scaring me.

The more sleep-deprived I became, the more emotional I got. I'd worked myself into a state of total fear. I tried to locate someone to come in to clear our home. She described this spirit, saying that he'd come from one of the local cemeteries. He hadn't been a nice person in real life; he'd been an alcoholic and a wife beater. Unfortunately, she couldn't clear the space for a few weeks, so she advised me to smudge every room in the house and to stop being so nice, to stop allowing it to be there. This confused me. I mean, aren't bad spirits in control? Apparently not. I was allowing this.

I finally had to pull it together, dig my way out of the fear and empower myself. I had to understand that the more I went to fear, the more I fed this negative spirit. Each time it spoke to me, I shut my channel down. I refused to engage in what I heard. I focused my energies on being strong and powerful. I sang empowering, positive songs. I smudged. I did whatever I could to keep the energy positive.

I energetically filled the room with light from Source because the negative cannot live within the positive. I even thanked it for helping me to learn how to empower myself, but now the learning was complete and he could go. It took a while because I didn't believe in myself without question, but then finally one day, the voice stopped. I was no longer amusing him so he went elsewhere.

The real test came when my husband went on another trip. Everything was fine. I didn't stand in fear and I slept well. There were no voices, nor were there any dreams where he invaded my channel.

From this experience, I learned that I hadn't been protecting myself fully. These are lessons for someone who is sensitive to energies and must learn, like any student, to handle them. This was also a lesson about me believing and trusting that I was protected, and trusting in myself and my own strength.

When I compare those two experiences, spaced three years apart, I most definitely passed the test this latter time. I hope you see in this lesson that sometimes the complete learning can come months, even years later. Sometimes learning comes in layers. With each lesson, you build on previous lessons until you've got it. Fully.

In our instant fix society, we run the risk thinking that lessons and healing need to be instantaneous. Yes, they can be if our thoughts and beliefs change instantly. Some people experience miracles because their beliefs change that rapidly. For others, it becomes a practice - plodding away with baby steps until the lesson is completed. There is no right way. There are no mistakes. We all learn differently, at different speeds.

Many people are freaked out about the idea of negative spirits, and Hollywood hasn't helped. Often people prefer to believe in, and focus on, positive spirits, while living in avoidance of the existence of negative spirits. However, we can't live in avoidance. Like everything in life, there is balance. We must have negative if we have positive. If we ignore the existence of the negative, then how can we experience life fully?

In real life, what do we do with negative people? We don't pretend they don't exist. We may not want to be around them but we can't deny their existence. It's no different with negative spirits. We might not want to call them to us, and we won't if we don't allow it to happen, but we can't deny their existence. Just like humans, it's important not to give power to the negative because the true power is in love. True power is in the light.

Chapter 9
A Lesson in Responsibility & Letting Go

One day Isa came to our session and mentioned that he was tired because a male father figure was in our home, connecting to him from spirit, and it felt like this spirit was related to my husband. It was my father-in-law, who'd recently passed. During our session, my father in law said he was worried about an older female with chest or lung issues. To prepare us, he said that she'd be passing in a short amount of time - within 3 months to 3 years - depending on free will.

Here are some myths about spirit mediums. We assume they know details, as if spirit is talking to them on a telephone. Rather, it's like speaking and translating a different language. Sometimes things can be difficult to retrieve or get lost in translation. This spirit couldn't communicate well in life nor in spirit so it was a challenge for Sheila to communicate with him.

Another thing you should know is that not all mediums retrieve information in the same way. This information was retrieved through pictures and feelings, so names were difficult to retrieve and sometimes it required piecing together bits of information.

Lastly, sometimes the information is just wrong or misleading on purpose. This isn't the medium's fault, unless of course they're fraudulent. However, sometimes the information they retrieve from spirit is channeled to assist us with our lessons. This happened to me several times and the messages were very powerful in pointing out emotions in my life that needed clearing.

As this spirit described an elderly woman about to pass, it struck me that my mother had lung and heart issues. But since this spirit was connected to my husband, it seemed more likely the information being presented concerned my mother-in-law. Since I was close to my mother-in-law, I wasn't happy with that scenario either. But I felt an intense moment of fear wondering if it would be my mother.

I'd spent my life in overwhelming fear of losing my loved ones. It controlled me daily and the fear ran so deep that I lived in avoidance of discussing death and loss. Now that there was no avoiding it, this didn't sit well with me. Not at all.

As mentioned earlier, Isa and my guides often had this dance where Isa would bring something up and then my guides would continue the theme. This could be quite uncomfortable yet profound for my learning. My hope is that, in due course, you too will see the beauty of this dance and how it was orchestrated for my benefit.

The previous week, Sheila and my guides had addressed my feelings of responsibility and guilt about my mother. I'd taken it upon myself that, as penance for wishing my mother would die when I was 12 years old, I would now be responsible for keeping her alive. During my journaling, I wrote:

> I'd come to believe I was responsible for my mother's accident and therefore I am responsible for all the bad things that happen to her in life. As a result, I've spent my entire life making sure that nothing bad happens to her. Protecting her. This was an enormous responsibility. I suddenly realize that I've allowed myself to be parentified. This realization stuns me because I understand that this cannot be a healthy attachment. My mother is not

my child. I cannot protect her. I cannot save her. Yet the idea of not being able to do so terrifies me.

How can I override God's plan? Someday something bad will happen - my mother is going to die - and I honestly have no idea how I will manage because I will have failed. I will have failed in a way that will never allow me to heal because the guilt will be too much to bear. I always say that when my parents die, I don't want to live with regrets or guilt. But I will, regardless, because guilt is so entwined with my relationship.

So, it's time for me to energetically cut the cords. Part of me panics because I'm afraid that my mother will die in the process and I will blame myself. But I trust that spirit will clear me of this guilt as I learn my lesson and move forward.

Sheila said that the illusion of responsibility is not reality. The reality is that we create our lessons in spirit before incarnating so when I feel the need to rescue or save someone, I'm impeding the other soul's learning. Rescuing a person is very different from empowering a person to help themselves.

Sheila helped me to understand that I'd spent many years wasting my energy through fear when nothing happened to my mother. She asked me:

How do you define "saving"? Does she have to live to 102? Eventually, we all die so she's going to pass and you'll say, "I couldn't save her". Technically, you've been working all along in fear trying to prevent her passing but your issues are Godly issues. You are not God. And just saying, "I wish you were dead," and then having that [accident] occur is a lesson in itself from spirit to recognize that you don't have that power. It's still the child taking responsibility and saying, "I made a mistake, I wasn't perfect, I failed and therefore I have to pay for the rest of my life."

It made me realize that the chronic fear of losing someone was infinitely worse than actually losing them because the heightened fear was destroying my body, my vitality and my life. That's not to minimize the trauma of losing a loved one because it's a very stressful thing to experience, but we experience death and then we know we must move on. On the other hand, I was reliving the possibility of death every single day for over 30 years. I lived every day as if the bottom would fall out of my life. A part of me wonders if my health issues were a subconscious attempt to beat everyone to the grave so I wouldn't have to face this fear.

Sheila wasn't kidding when she said:

> The Universe is going to prepare you because you need to understand that it's okay for her to go and it's not your responsibility. God or Source decides that, not you, and you need to clear this now because when it's time for her to go, you can't be saying, "I'm responsible for the fact that she left, I couldn't save her and that's why she died."

My guides added that:

> It doesn't have to be a traumatic state of life, but it has been for you and we're saying, change it! It doesn't have to be that way. Why are you living your life that way? Why not live your life in peace and happiness?

Sheila asked me to think about all the time I'd spent trying to be responsible for everything in my life and how much time I've actually missed out on living and experiencing. "You always give up something to be responsible so you're giving up time for your own enjoyment".

My guides asked me, "What would happen if you only had a few days to live"? I said I wasn't afraid of dying. They responded that I had no fear of death because it doesn't matter. I didn't have any wishes, dreams or needs but to be responsible for somebody else. They said, "You're avoiding your wishes, wants and needs".

I replied with a sarcastic laugh, saying, "Nice! I always thought I was happy before I started this journey. Now I'm not happy! At least I can laugh about it! Thanks for putting that into perspective for me!"

Sheila tried to help clarify:

> What they're saying is that you weren't actually happy, you were standing in the illusion of being happy. When you walk through this lesson, you're going to actually have true happiness, not fake happiness, not delusional happiness. It's reality.
>
> When you're standing in the illusion of happiness and thinking that you're happy, are you actually happy? Do we ever ask ourselves that? I feel happy right now but am I really happy? Or is that the illusion of being happy? And why am I happy? Is it for myself or somebody else? True happiness comes from within. Now, if you feed off other people making you happy, that's not true happiness and that will only last as long as they're happy.
>
> So, this is why you have the fear of loss. It

comes all the way back around to fear because you think that your happiness is tied to other people. If they are not alive, then you have no happiness, and then you have no reason to live. That's the core.

I went home with a lot to absorb. It would take me several weeks to process, given that the core beliefs were so strong.

The following week, I had a surreal experience as I was waking up. I could analyze what was occurring, making me believe that it was more than a dream. It felt like a message. I met my mother's soul and she was standing at the end of my bed. It wasn't my mother in physical form. She was formed in bright light with faint outlines and her mouth was just a black hole. I found it somewhat disturbing, but not frightening, just weird.

I could feel her pain. She'd been suffering from fractured ribs, a side effect of Osteoarthritis of the spine. I told her that I release her. She thanked me but said she couldn't be fully released energetically because my brother, Brian, couldn't release her. This surprised me but on later reflection, I knew it was true. She told me that she would come back as a white dog. Upon waking, I thought I'd had a nightmare, until I realized I'd felt complete love and compassion. I felt peace.

Recounting this with Sheila made me shiver. Shivering had become a form of communication with my guides when they wanted to show me confirmation. Sheila said my subconscious initiated the encounter and took care of it so I could heal myself.

In the next breath, I hesitatingly said, "I don't want to say it, but I have to. I think part of me realizes that my father-in-law is talking about my mom. That's what I had to face this week". The

Universe concurred. I started shaking. I think I was hoping to be wrong. I realized that I'd released my mother, but on a selfish, human level, I hadn't.

Sheila said:

> She's lived her life and done what she's wanted to do and now if she wants to go, she has every right. It would be no different if you wanted to cross but somebody was holding you here. You wouldn't want that; you'd want them to respect your decision. True love is about that, about accepting and allowing. Now it's about processing and preparing for it so that you're not overwhelmed when it actually occurs.

As we discussed the process of accepting and preparing, Sheila said that the next step would be to have a conversation with my mother about death, and my acceptance of her passing.

My guides said, "Everything that you've learned spiritually up until this point is for this purpose, is for the purpose of coming to terms/acceptance of your parents passing."

Sheila joined in, saying:

> It's the ultimate test of your spiritual belief. How much do you believe in the stuff you've been learning? Because if you believe it properly and fully, then their passing will hurt you on a human level only because you'll feel sad to see them go, but you'll rejoice for their spirit.

I think back to all the times I'd wanted to run from facing my fears, and this was probably my biggest challenge of all. Worst of all, it was something I couldn't run from. I'd reached the end of the line and I was being forced to face facts. This was probably the hardest week of my life, having confirmation that it would be my mother passing. I grieved for a week. I couldn't stop crying, the emotion purging from me.

Eventually, thinking about Sheila saying that I'd always have contact with my mother in spirit allowed me to begin feeling more at peace. But I wasn't completely over it. I still found myself crying at the sound of a sad song or for no reason at all. Eventually, I found the strength to move on. It didn't happen overnight, but in baby steps.

I phoned my mom and we had a sweet, emotional conversation about her dying. Sadly, I learned that she was afraid of dying. Her strict religious beliefs in which everyone is considered a sinner made her question her fate after passing. I realized in that moment that I was supposed to help her pass. In just accepting, I assisted her, whereas before I had been isolating her in my resistance and denial, not wanting to speak about her dying. I was there for her in a genuine way, not with the need to fix or save, but I was just there to listen. It felt good.

During our next session, Isa sweetly let me know that my mom would see her next birthday, seven months away. Moments later, Sheila informed me that a man fitting my maternal grandfather's description had appeared from spirit. Sheila channeled him, saying he and many others will be there to greet my mother when it's her time to cross and for me not to worry. It'll be like a reunion. He said:

> If you can imagine that she's coming over to a surprise party then that will hopefully make you feel better, because that's what we're planning. As soon as your mom crosses she won't have time to think about not being

alive because we've got so much for her to do.

My grandfather wanted to reassure me that my mother's passing would be beautiful. He said:

> I'll make sure that all this will happen and we're very excited. When it's time for your mother to cross, if you would look at it like you're gifting her to us, then that would mean the world to me.

He said to tell my mom, "You've got this, you can do this! We are far from done when we pass, far from done and I'm so excited to prove that to her." With that, he gave a rolling hand gesture with a bow and said goodbye.

Three months later, my mother-in-law was admitted to the hospital and diagnosed with ovarian cancer. She passed away within 18 months of my father-in-law's message from spirit.

The universe had misled me with purpose over a 4-week period to help me through this important hurdle in my life. I've had some monumental teachings in the seven years of my spiritual guidance, but none as profound as this. Had I not processed this learning, I know that my mother's passing would have wounded me to my soul. I know that had I not "passed" this test, I'd be stuck, unable to move forward in my spiritual evolution.

My father passed away in April, 2017 from Alzheimer's. Before his passing, my paternal grandmother in spirit asked me to connect with my father's spirit to help him as he was afraid to pass. I assisted his soul in finding the peace to cross. When I heard of his passing, I felt relief. I wasn't devastated, I was grateful that he graduated out of this life to go home. Sheila channeled him after his passing and I cried with joy at how happy he was to have crossed.

Just days before the launch of this book, in March 2018, my mom passed away peacefully at the age of 94. It felt like the book had been delayed until this final chapter in my life was complete. My mother had been frail and unwell, hanging onto life out of fear.

Five months previous to her passing, we had a heartfelt, tearful talk. I told her it was okay to pass. She said she wanted to go but she loses her faith. We talked about how my father was at peace. We also talked about my strong faith. As a result, she felt at peace. We discussed many things, including our love for one another, then we hugged.

Mom finally made the transition and I was ok. I felt immense relief that she was finally in a better place. Sheila channelled her the day of her passing and she was happy. My mother stated that her father had come by and convinced her to cross.

From such a painful lesson that started years ago came peace. I was able to follow through on my grandfather's request to look at my mother's passing as gifting her to him. As I write about it the day after her passing, part of me feels loss because losing my parents is the end of a chapter in my life, but I'm ok. With endings come new beginnings.

Chapter 10
A Lesson in Acceptance

Isa had warned me. He'd developed colitis for the first time, passing bloody stool. We were 11 months into our work so he was supposed to be getting better, not worse, from my perspective, at least! From his perspective, he'd keep getting worse until I learned my lessons.

Isa said I was feeling depressed and heavy, and I was very much in my head. He felt that I was sitting in things too long, not living, that I obsessed in one direction or the other, so he was trying to get me to create more balance.

This was the roller coaster of our relationship. Isa would try to help me heal, so he'd get sick to reflect my own state, then I'd get upset because he was sick, which would make him sicker.

I told Sheila that I was so heavy because he's sick. I told her that, "My heart just breaks because I know he's getting sick because of me and it's not fair to him." In the next breath, I said, "Maybe my lesson is to let him go, give him away."

Sheila said:

> You can't dishonor what he's doing for you. If you don't have him, then another animal or something else has to manifest instead to show you. He's come here specifically to help you, so if you dishonor his journey or send him somewhere else, he's saying, "Wait a second, I came here for you, now I don't have any life purpose". Then he'll go, he'll just die, and fast! His life purpose is to be with you. Even though you think he's suffering, it's his choice.

I reflected on this. Imagine a dog coming to Earth to assist you in healing and you just want to give him away? I thought I was loving him enough to give him away, but from Isa's perspective, he felt dismissed. What a lesson.

As I cried, I asked Sheila how to stop him from breaking my heart. She said that I need to come from the spiritual side of things, just like I could with my past lives. She added, "You were able to justify your past lives. It hurts for a while but then you get it. It's the same thing with animals. They have their purpose as well."

My guides also chimed in that, as I was facing the concept of my mother's passing, I also needed to look at Isa's mortality and understand what that meant. Letting that go is very important, to say, "Okay, it's going to be very sad whenever it happens, but I can handle it."

This was a hard lesson that would take some time to fully integrate. In the past, every time Isa got sick, I'd rush to the vet in fear. It was hard on me. It was hard on Isa. Now Isa had just upped the ante, getting attacks of colitis. He had an attack just the week before I was supposed to leave for a trip. If he hadn't improved, I would have canceled my trip.

I'd been consumed with Isa's health, which was only making me spin in the same cycle, making him sicker. I finally realized that I'd have to detach. I can love him, but I must honor his choices. Instead, I was trying to control his choices. If he chooses to get sick to assist me, then that's his choice. I might not like it or agree with it, but I dishonor him by my lack of acceptance. The only choice I could make that honors his journey is to step back from the emotion and analyze my definition of love.

Is spiritual love different from human love? You bet. I was attaching conditions with Isa. To show my love for him, I had to stand in fear and worry because that's how we're taught to nurture. I believed that if he loved me, he wouldn't choose to get sick because getting sick was taking him one step closer to death. My happiness was tied up in his being alive. I didn't want him to leave me.

True spiritual love is about honoring our choices and those of people around us. It's not about controlling people for our own happiness. Love and happiness are found within. True love is honoring someone else's lessons. It's allowing them to make their mistakes, if necessary, and grow from them. It's not about stepping in and fixing their lessons for them. There's no growth in that. It's about standing back and allowing. True spiritual love is unconditional but because we're constrained by our egos, it's something we humans struggle to conceive, never mind attain.

One day I let it all out. I cried away my fears and worries about losing Isa and came to an understanding that I can't run to the vet every time Isa gets sick. If Isa chooses to harm himself to assist me, then I accept. I may not like it, but I would no longer stand in the fear I was cycling in.

Two weeks later, Isa thanked me. He said he was happy that I was finally getting it, finally understanding where he was trying to take me. He said he was excited and felt a lot lighter because I was coming to some very clear realizations. He thanked me again the following week for not stressing out in any way connected to him. He didn't think I was going to extremes like I had previously, and felt as if I was more stable with him.

I had to admit, I felt better too. That's the funny thing about stepping through fear. It always feels better on the other side.

Chapter 11
A Lesson in Trust

Not long after, Isa told me I was being stubborn, that I needed to let go of control and allow myself to be guided. He told me I was swimming against the current.

This was a concept I struggled with. Isa said I tried too hard and when I'm trying too hard, I'm trying to take control. Isa explained that the easiest way to understand control is that when you do something and it's not flowing, you aren't going with the spiritual flow. When you feel like you're going against the flow, you're trying to take control. To assist my learning, Isa wanted me to pay more attention to the daily direction I got from my guides.

This was true. In hindsight, how many times had I tried doing something to find myself blocked? Things would go wrong and I'd feel the block in the energy, like hitting a brick wall. I'm a doer and I'm stubborn. I'll try something until it figuratively kills me.

Instead of going with the universal flow, I'd try to plow through the block, getting frustrated in the process, and no matter what I'd do, it would never work out. I'd end up having to go in a different direction in the end after I'd exhausted myself in the process. Instead, I should have said "Maybe it's not meant to be. Maybe I need to go in a different direction." Isa was asking me to do this instead of controlling.

Isa suggested, instead of swimming upstream, against the current, that I do a meditation before bedtime. Imagine myself on a raft going down the lazy river, paying attention to the trees, the sun, the animals, just enjoying the moment and letting the raft take me down the river. If I do that meditation, he said, I'd be telling my subconscious to go with the flow.

Isa also explained that when I feel blocked, I need to say to the Universe, "If this is not meant to be, fine. I'm going to try this one more time and if it's supposed to happen, please help me. However, if there is a block, I'll move on." I was to take their guidance and stay in peace instead of getting frustrated and exhausted trying to do something that wasn't meant to be.

The Universe speaks to us all the time. We don't have to be mediums for the Universe to talk to us. We just need to pay attention. Most of us are so busy with our lives that we don't stand in the moment and pay attention to what is around us. If we pay attention, the universe talks to us through other people, animals, and different scenarios. Have you ever heard several people tell you the same thing and then discount what was said? Pay attention to the message because there's guidance in it. This was a process that the Universe taught me. Just walk the path they show you.

Two profound examples of this guidance stand out in my mind. The first was walking through fear, following the guidance of the Universe. The second was following the signs from the Universe to get me to a specific place.

In this first example, I was being asked to trust in a big way. Much to the chagrin of my conventional physician husband, I didn't believe in vaccinations. It started when our first dog, Misha, developed a life-threatening condition called hemolytic anemia, an autoimmune disorder in which the immune system attacks the red blood cells. As I later discovered, animals are over vaccinated, especially small ones, and this life-threatening condition was just one side effect. Misha's situation was so acute that he required a blood transfusion. The vet prepared us for the worst since there was a good chance Misha might die while waiting for the blood to arrive, or from the blood transfusion itself.

Misha made it through the blood transfusion, but he wasn't out of the woods. We had to put him on chemotherapy and high dose steroids to suppress his immune system, to give his body the chance to start making red blood cells without attacking them. We got lucky. He recovered. Due to his history, he was no longer able to receive vaccinations other than rabies, which was required by law.

Fast forward to Isa. He was vaccinated as a puppy, but by the next spring, the conventional vet decided not to vaccinate him because he wasn't well enough. Over the next few months, I decided that, given his condition, I wouldn't vaccinate Isa unless necessary. Then I heard from our holistic vet that I could titer him instead, which entails a blood test to measure antibodies in the blood. This seemed like a good alternative and gave me some peace knowing that it was a viable option.

By the third spring, Isa's physical was due and I needed to ask my conventional vet to get Isa titered. My husband decided to come with me and the reason soon became apparent. He believed Isa should be vaccinated, that he couldn't live with himself if Isa contracted a life-threatening disease because of not being vaccinated. On the other hand, I couldn't live with myself if I had Isa vaccinated, and just like our first dog, had a life-threatening side effect from the vaccination. We found ourselves on opposite sides of the boxing ring, albeit amicable, with our conventional vet as the biased referee. I felt outnumbered.

My husband asked our vet if titering was effective and he explained why it wasn't. I learned that there is strong disagreement between conventional and holistic veterinary medicine. I was left in a quandary.

This quandary wormed itself into my meditation. As I got deep into one of my meditations, my conventional vet appeared in my mind saying, trust me. I hadn't experienced anything like this during my meditations so I couldn't shake the words. They had great meaning.

Like everything in my life at that point, this was a lesson in trust. I'd been trying to make the right decision based on hours of research, but, Sheila was suggesting I do something completely foreign. She was asking me to trust the Universe, that it would help me choose the right path, which would become apparent through my intuition if I could stand out of my fear and let the intuition in.

But what does the right path mean? To my mind, the right path meant working out perfectly, making me happy, all tied up in a pretty bow. To spirit, the right path meant taking me where I needed to go for my learning. I was trying to protect Isa, but something bad might have to happen to get me to a space I needed to be. Sheila added that, if you trust yourself and something bad happens, it doesn't mean you've made the wrong choice. You still made the right choice because the Universe, your soul, wants to take you on that path for a reason.

It was hard to wrap my head around this concept. It's a very difficult place to be, feeling you might be putting a person or animal at risk by trusting in the Universe. The responsibility feels huge.

Sheila repeated, "It doesn't mean that the outcome is going to be positive or good, it's going to be whatever it needs to be. It's like the Universe says:

You can't make mistakes. If you move, we will move you to where you need to go. The only problem is when you stand still and we can't move you, then nothing happens but stagnation.

That's where I was. I was stagnating and avoiding and the Universe was making me feel it ten-fold, trying to force me out of my indecision. I worked myself up into such a state that each time I brought Isa to play-school, I was afraid he would catch a life-threatening disease. It was irrational. I was feeling torn in my indecision so I did one of the most difficult things I've ever had to do. I considered getting Isa vaccinated.

I said to the Universe, "When I call the vet for an appointment, if it's in Isa's highest good to get vaccinated, the staff will answer the phone." You can't imagine my disappointment when they answered. With a racing heart and a sinking feeling, I booked the appointment. I asked the Universe again, "If it's not in Isa's highest good to get vaccinated, then have Isa vomit in front of me the morning of his appointment." It's kind of a harsh thing to ask, given Isa's history of vomiting, but the vet won't vaccinate a sick dog and I wanted to ensure he was healthy enough for the vaccines.

The morning of Isa's appointment arrived. I don't think I'll ever forget the look in Isa's eyes just before he vomited. It was like he was saying, "Are you paying attention?" I had my answer. I called the vet's office and rescheduled his appointment. Then, I asked the same of the Universe: "Have Isa vomit in front of me the morning of his appointment if vaccinating him isn't in his highest good. If he vomits again, I won't vaccinate him at all." The day finally came and Isa didn't vomit.

I buckled Isa into the back seat of the car, then got into the driver's seat but couldn't move. I was terrified and felt on the verge of a panic attack. In that moment, I completely understood why my first dog got hemolytic anemia. It was to take me to this space in time because this was probably the greatest spiritual test that could be asked of me. This little dog had sacrificed so much to help me heal and maybe he was sacrificing himself yet again. It was a test of faith.

As I tried to pull myself together, I kept repeating "I am not praying to the god of fear, you have no power over me. I listen to guidance from the Universe." The fear wouldn't subside. I didn't know what to do. I remembered that when the path doesn't feel comfortable, my guides would take me to the place I needed to go. Just listen to my intuition. But how could I hear my intuition in so much fear? So, I said out loud to my guides, "I feel sick to my stomach because of this fear. How am I supposed to be guided?" I pleaded with them for help and drove towards, what felt to me, like a firing squad.

I nervously waited for the vet to come into the exam room. I think he's one of the kindest people, except that we find ourselves on opposite sides of the fence where it comes to vaccines. When the vet walked into the room, either my guides directed him to help me or he could see it in my demeanor. Whatever the case, he talked to me about the old vaccination schedules and how dogs were over-vaccinated and he compared the old protocols to the new ones. And the more he talked in his calming manner, the more I felt my fear subside.

It happened. I was finally able to step outside my intense fear and feel my intuition. My intuition was saying to get Isa vaccinated.

I said to myself, "It is in God's hands", and I handed over my beloved dog into the vet's arms all the while thanking the vaccines for keeping Isa protected from disease. I walked through the fear I had been avoiding for two years and it was an enormous relief having made the decision.

After Isa's appointment, as I sat in my car, preparing to drive home, I felt so empowered having walked through my fear. I was proud of myself. I'll never forget what happened after that. As crazy as it sounds, I felt one of my guides holding my right hand, our fingers entwined, as if to say, "You did well. It's okay". I had felt them touching my upper back before, but I had never felt such a loving touch in my life. It made me cry. As I cried, I kept looking at my hand, hoping that the sensation would never disappear, hoping that I would never forget the day that I completely surrendered in trust to the Universe.

Two years later when Isa was due for his vaccinations, I left the decision up to him. He could communicate with me so why would I take responsibility for such an important decision, especially since my husband and I were on opposite sides of the fence? Isa decided that he didn't want to see the conventional vet because he was happy with his holistic vet, Dr. Haighaght (pronounced Hyatt). He felt that if he were vaccinated, his immune system would not respond well and since he was doing well at the time, it would throw him off. We decided to get him titered instead. I must admit, I was relieved.

******

The second profound example of following the signs of spiritual guidance occurred last summer. It was a Friday and I'd been overly stressed with work. To recharge, my guides told me I needed to go that very day for a weekend trip by myself. I had no idea where to go. The one place recommended to me was booked up so I found myself feeling rushed for time without a plan. I asked the Universe to find me a place on the internet. I found a place, and within a couple of hours I was on my way to a summer weekend getaway. This was so unlike me. I like to plan, but instead I was forced to trust.

The following morning, I walked into town to buy some water when I noticed a bunch of people standing around some structure. I went to investigate. I'd been guided to Lock 45 in Port Severn, one of the locks on the Trent-Severn Waterway. This 240-mile waterway connects Georgina Bay to Lake Ontario via 44 locks and I was there to celebrate their 100th anniversary. I completely forgot what I'd gone into town for, mesmerized by the boats coming and going through the lock. I spent two days watching those boats, becoming one with the water. When I wasn't at the lock, I sat on a floating dock at my hotel. With every passing minute, I felt my stress melting away from me. I came home completely rejuvenated, something I hadn't experienced in quite some time.

I knew this was my means to de-stress. I could feel it in my soul, the need to be on the water. When I came home, I told my husband I was buying a boat. He was shocked because "impulsive" was not me. I'd never even driven a boat. Where would I find one? What if I didn't like boating? The list of reasonable objections went on, but I felt like I'd been guided and now I was just following that guidance. I was going to buy a boat.

I found a used boat and put a down payment on it, but afterwards, I wasn't sure that it was the right boat for me. It was a 23-foot speed-boat so it had no rails on it. Big rails around this boat would ruin the look of it, according to the salesman. I emailed him, saying that I'd reconsidered, that I wasn't sure it was the right boat for me. Considering that I'd be on this boat alone, I needed to ensure my safety.

Within moments of sending that email, I drove to the grocery store, down the same street I'd driven thousands of times over the past 25 years. I saw the same boat parked in someone's driveway. It had small profile rails on it down the front center of the boat instead of encircled around it. I'd been paying attention and received a very clear message from the Universe. I came home after getting my groceries and found pictures of this boat with small profile rails on it. I asked the marine salesman if he could put rails on it and he said he knew someone who could, so I bought the boat.

Everything just flowed, from the moment I was guided to go away up until buying my boat. It was a plan to take me to a place that feeds my soul. The Universe knew what I needed and they laid out the path for me. All I had to do was see the signs.

I hope you can better understand how the Universe works to help us in moving with the flow of spirit. It's a difficult concept to grasp because we don't stand in awareness of the things that happen around us. If you just pay attention, you will see the synchronicity.

Chapter 12
Layers

It was probably nine months into my spiritual journey, exactly four years after my latest health crisis, when my health issues resurfaced. It was shocking how quickly it triggered the feelings of depression and hopelessness that I'd felt four years previous.

At the time, I wrote in my journal:

> It's not as if I'd survived cancer yet I still feel like a cancer survivor. My life, both physically and emotionally, has been marked by that illness that has no name. To this day, my life is defined "before my illness" and "after my illness," not because I want to hold onto it, but because it was such a life-changing event. I'm a different person today than I was before I got sick.

> So, I sit here trying to sort out my lessons. I realize that not having a diagnosis for my illness four years ago has never brought me closure, making it difficult to completely move forward. I thought I had, but it's evident to me now that I haven't.

Even though I'd healed myself, it was clear that I had unresolved emotional issues and fears connected to my illness.

As we processed this learning, Sheila said:

> Your lesson is about balance; finding balance on many levels, balancing the body, balancing holistic and allopathic healing, balancing your stress levels, balancing your worry, and balancing your fear. It's balance all over the place.

My guides also said:

> You've come this far. Don't forget where you came
> from. Give yourself some credit for what you've done,
> but look and remember how it got you to that place the
> last time and don't make those same mistakes again.

When I asked what mistakes, Sheila replied, "Fear. Fear of many things".

This was the exact scenario I was facing in the moment. I was sensitive to medications and had found myself resorting to taking pharmaceutical medications because holistic alternatives weren't helping me. I found myself in fear of further damaging my body.

Here I found myself in the same scenario I'd found myself with Isa's dilemma around vaccinations. I was being asked to trust, to ask the Universe to assist me with a holistic solution, and if it didn't work within a specified time frame, then to trust and go the conventional route.

My guides wanted me to empower myself by paying attention and seeing the signs. They wanted me to discern on my own, through my own intuition and presence, to make decisions on my own and to trust them. Trust myself. Instead, I was in a place of fear avoiding medications because I was afraid of the past.

I asked my guides what was wrong with me when I got my mystery illness. They wouldn't tell me. Their reply was, "What's important is the process of how you came through the sickness, not the disease itself". I was supposed to help myself by not having a diagnosis. It would have been too easy to hand over my power to a health professional had I been given a label for what ailed me.

Without a label, I could second-guess myself and my sanity. I had to find trust in myself. Not having a label didn't allow me to have awareness or control over my mystery illness because I had no gauge of comparison like we have with diseases. Was this a one-time thing or would I never heal? As a result, each time I'd have a detox reaction, some of them quite scary, I'd go to uncertainty and fear that my illness was worsening. Or later after I'd healed, if I got sick, I'd go to fear, wondering if my illness was recurring.

What I realized in that moment is that not having a label was a tool for my learning. I could learn through uncertainty and in that uncertainty, I could empower myself to heal. I suppose it's no different than someone who heals from cancer naturally. You choose to follow a path less traveled, breaking new ground. It's that process that is very empowering to them because they did it their own way, with the strength of their own mind and the strength of their own will. In that same way, I had to face the strength of my own will to live.

My illness was a gift in so many ways. It made me draw strength from places I never thought possible, when all I wanted to do was just lie down and die because that was the easiest way out. Moving forward, the biggest and most difficult lesson for me would be finding balance in my life to prevent further illness. It's no coincidence that the health issues that most plagued me are endocrine issues. The endocrine system is all about balance, homeostasis. Health is energy and negative energy, or fear, is illness. The way to eradicate fear and resistance is through trust - trusting ourselves, trusting the intelligence of the Universe, and trusting the intelligence of our journey.

As Sheila said:

> It's a constant battle between your ego and your spirit so
> your ego creates the fear and your spirit stays in peace
> and trust. This battle has been a continuous progression
> throughout your whole life. That's why we live, to create
> the balance and when there's an imbalance, we're learn-
> ing a lesson. When you find balance again, you're in
> peace and then the Universe provides something else and
> you learn another lesson.

There were many layers to my learning around fear of illness.
It didn't just disappear in that moment. I learned and grew from
that experience, but it's easy not to be fearful about getting sick
when you're rested or not stressed out. I would then have a
period in which I would be sleep-deprived for weeks on end and
the bar would get raised. How would I handle illness when my
defenses were down?

I've never faced illness like I did back in 2008, but I came to
learn that my soul wanted to assist others to heal, and the way I
could assist them is through experience. I needed to honor my
soul's path, although it took me some time to reach that acceptance. In fact, I had to work on forgiving myself for hating my
soul for wanting this experience. Self-love runs very deep, down
to the level of loving and accepting our soul's path, no matter
what it may be. It's a difficult concept for many, to honor the
challenges we're faced with.

Years later, as illness surfaced again, my guides said that my
"mystery illness" would never get a label because it hadn't ex-
isted in anyone else before. They said my illness was an accumulation of other diseases, similar but not quite the same and it lies
dormant in the cells, perhaps cellular memory, getting triggered

by stress.

As Sheila said, from a spiritual perspective, it was a trigger, so who cares? However, I never understood why my blood work kept coming back normal when I felt every part of me shutting down. Sheila said, "That's what happens when spirit intervenes. It looks normal, but it's not." Sheila was right. Had my blood work been abnormal, it would have taken me down a completely different path - a path to conventional medicine. It was the stepping stone to my current path.

Whichever way you look at my illness, there's always a different way to view it. Like a kaleidoscope, with each view, I gain new understanding and gratitude, but sometimes I need to go to the depths of despair to get there. The last time I faced illness, in a state of severe sleep deprivation, I said I'd check out instead of fighting but I always seemed to find the strength to deal with it, to move on. I always found a way to fight the fear. I might not land on my feet perfectly, but that's not the end goal. The end goal is that I try and with each attempt, I learn and heal.

I'd like to say, "Practice makes perfect" but the spiritual journey is not about perfection. It's about practice. With each attempt, there is growth and evolution. If it takes one attempt, that's great; if it takes 100 attempts, then that's great too. What matters is that you try.

Spirituality isn't about showing up at church every Sunday and being absolved of so-called sins, admitting you're a bad person - a sinner - then repeating the ritual every week. Then you go home and do the same things all over again. Where is the growth in that? That's just a distraction, an avoidance, and there is no self-love in that.

Spirituality is about showing up and taking responsibility for your life, your soul and your journey. It's about digging into the self, knowing the self, facing your fears, your shadows, and your challenges. It's the seed for change, growth, and finding peace within. It is hard work, but rewarding.

Chapter 13
A Lesson in Self-Awareness

About a year into our work together, Isa told me that in August I'd be taking a course and he was very excited for me about it, that it was a step in the right direction. This workshop would be around the time of a family member's birthday in August. As was the dance between my guides and Isa, my guides also told me a week later that, "A trip to a hotel will prove to be a necessary one. We suggest you release all your worries and inhibitions for this event."

As it turned out, my massage therapist had loaned me a book written by a famous medical intuitive. The following week, I went to her website, and lo and behold, she was giving a weekend workshop in my area in August, two days before my niece's birthday, so I signed up for the course.

There were so many lessons for me because of that seminar, but one of the greatest lessons was about self-awareness and "holding your space". The Universe had placed me in an environment of 64 other people where negative aspects, termed "lower vibration frequencies", were the focus. Not that people were low vibrational frequencies, but that the topics were around negative aspects or emotions such as alcoholism, fears, sadness, lack of self-worth, betrayal, and guilt.

The medical intuitive had read the energetic fields of several people during the workshop. I had found myself crying empathically for people on several occasions and found myself quite drained by the end.

Sheila said:

> No matter how much we all come from the heart, come
> from peace, you need to learn how to sit in low vibra-
> tional frequency but not come down to that level. If you
> lower your vibrational frequency, it increases every-
> body's low vibrational frequency. It's like if you have
> high vibrational frequency [positive topics or emotions]
> and your intention is prayer, joy, and happiness and it
> builds up to be bigger joy, bigger prayer, bigger positive.
> However, if you put a whole bunch of negative in a pile,
> it's a bigger negative.

I understood the concept but didn't understand how to put it into
practice. Sheila told me to remove myself from the emotion and
stand in high vibrational frequency or positive emotion. I felt
kind of obtuse because I couldn't understand how to do that.

Sheila said:

> The key is that it's the empath in you. What does an
> empath do? An empath picks up the energies from other
> people and takes them on for themselves. When you're
> not aware of that, then you allow your energy to be
> manipulated. You feel for others so you felt for others so
> much that you're adding to their pile of negativity, mak-
> ing their low vibration bigger.

I'd never thought about it. I'd been conditioned that when
someone is discussing "negative" topics, I would bring myself to
the same space, meaning I'd drain myself of my own energy to
bring myself to their low vibration. I've been told I'm an empath,
but I never really knew the implications of it. I thought I felt for
people. What it really means is that I sacrifice myself for people.

Sheila added that:

> I can feel for you and empathize with you, but I don't
> need to go sit in it. I can control the amount I feel. I can
> observe it and allow it to touch me enough to allow me
> to assist but I'm not going to let it consume me or take
> over my energy or bring my energy to a different level
> because I'm not helping you at all. If I come down to
> another's level, that's not helping.
>
> This is a lesson for a healer. You want to hold the space
> with positive energy. You don't want to feed into the
> negative. I don't want to go, "Poor you, that's so sad".
> I want to say, "Let's honor that, let's honor that you felt
> fearful". We can honor that and respect it, but how do we
> get you the hell out of there? I don't want to go, "Yeah,
> part of me is fearful so let me go stand with you in that
> one", and we can both look at it and feel bad.
>
> Why do you need to learn that? Because when you're
> working one-on-one with somebody or in a group, you
> need to hold the space as positive.

This was my lesson in a powerful way. I'd been told my destiny
was to be a healer, yet I'd burned out as a social worker. As an
empath, I'd never been taught to feel without holding onto the
emotion. I thought everyone was an empath.

Sheila told me a story about a dog at a shelter not allowing
anyone to touch him. When he communicated to Sheila, he explained that when people pity him, it makes him angry because
it weakens him. It makes him feel worse. Sheila explained that
it's not love and it's not compassion. She added that, "Sometimes
people who are in a place of victim attract pity to them, which
makes them even weaker so they're really self-sabotaging."

That was a pivotal moment. I realized that I'd felt the same way when I was sick and had nothing left in me. I clearly remembered not being able to speak with my mother because her fear, pity and concern, although required of a mother by society's standards, would take away every last ounce of my energy, leaving me feeling closer to death. No one wins.

Contrast that with my husband who is empathetic, but he always held a positive space because he knew it was what I needed. My energy was always neutral/positive with him. I gravitated towards his positive energy because it energized me.

No wonder, as an empath, I've struggled with my health. My belief system had been programmed that, to love, I needed to feel deeply and take it on. It's no wonder I'd spent so many years of my life blocking or avoiding my feelings, pushing them down, so I wouldn't have to feel them. What I should have been doing was releasing them right away instead of burying the feelings within my cells which would ultimately ruin my health.

This is a powerful lesson for everyone. It's a core value our society is taught. It "proves" that we love another when in fact it's not love. How can it be love if it leaves a person still feeling like a victim? How can it be love if we haven't assisted that person in moving forward, empowering themselves? How can it be love if we avoid speaking the truth, instead feeding into the illusions of the victim? The victim wants pity because then nothing can change. The victim doesn't want to leave an abusive partner, or stop drinking or feel gratitude for any given moment. Feeling pity is neither love nor self-love. Rather, love and self-love provide the opportunities for growth and evolution.

Love is also about honoring and accepting the choices of others. It's the free will right of every person to choose for themselves how they wish to live their life. If they choose to live from the perspective of a victim, it's their choice and you must honor it. After all, we're culturally programmed to be victims and our growth is in coming out of victim-ness and standing on our own, knowing that we always have the choice to change, be strong, and empowered. That is love, to honor their decision while at the same time not pitying them. You can honor and accept another's choice without condoning their behavior. You can love while at the same time step away, not putting your energy into controlling or changing the other.

Sometimes love is making the choice to leave a situation to honor that other person's choice. We have a hard time with this concept in our society. The hardest thing is to let go emotionally. We want to control, to fix, to give ultimatums, or to stomp our feet in frustration because the other won't change. Then finally after years of fighting, we might finally let go of the situation because we have nothing left to give or we become bitter because we've tried to live someone else's life instead of our own.

Loving another while honoring their choices is unconditional love. Is it attainable in our lifetime? Perhaps not. Is it what we should strive towards? Absolutely. Who we really are is love and peace, but it's clouded by the ego, who wants to control. It's only by living our lives with unconditional love that we find happiness and peace within ourselves and society. It's the key to living in harmony.

Chapter 14
A Lesson in Soul Groups

According to my guides, it was time for another regression to explore another past life that had been superimposed on my current life as Wanda. It was a life that was impacting my current life.

During this past life regression, I learned that I was also married to a doctor, with two small children and that he was murdered when they were young. Two years later, I was still mourning my husband's death. To compound things, I'd been left without any money to care for our children. We were eventually forced to live and work on the streets. My children were taken from me and my sorrowful life ended when I hung myself.

During my regression, my neck started to hurt and I saw myself hanging from a beam in the ceiling. Oddly enough, I'd woken up that morning with a stiff neck. I've been plagued by neck issues my entire life, perhaps cellular memory from this past life?

Sheila was directed to take me to the time of my death and walk me through passing from my life into spirit. She asked me who had come to assist me pass over. I began sobbing. It was Norm, my current husband. I knew then that he'd been my husband in that past life as well.

It also explained my intense fear of Norm dying in this life. I'd break out in a cold sweat if he was running late, thinking he was lying dead in a ditch, or had come to some other tragic end. It tormented me. Now I understood the connection between my past life and my intense fear in this life. The emotions we experience in a past life often come through from our soul, which holds all our past life experience and trauma, to be cleared in a current life.

As a result of this awareness, I cleared my intense fear of Norm dying. It was such a relief to no longer be crippled by this fear. I really didn't understand at the time how much energy went into feeding that fear. However, it left me wondering about the identities of those two children in my past life. My guides indicated that those two souls were connected to me in this life but they would not blindly give me the answer. The information would come to me intuitively, just as it had with Isa.

A couple of months after this regression, I was detoxing when I suddenly experienced an all-knowing feeling. My massage therapist had been one of my children from this past life. My whole body shivered with confirmation as the pieces fell into place.

Brian had been my massage therapist for about 12 years. From our first meeting, I felt a special connection with him. That is, after my initial fear subsided that this man could break me in two. Brian is big. He's tall and he's a body builder, however, he has a beautiful, soft energy about him. I never understood this connection. I just felt as if I'd known him my entire life. We quickly learned we had a common goal around holistic health. My fibromyalgia brought me to his office for a massage at least weekly. The time would fly by as we discussed different things we'd learned from our individual research.

Once I fully comprehended that Brian was our son in this past life, it all began to make sense. Had I not had fibromyalgia, I would never have connected with Brian in this life. It had a spiritual purpose. I also realized that the connection I felt with him was a soul-group connection, even a mother-child connection coming through from my past life. My guides later confirmed through Sheila that Brian and I had shared many lifetimes together.

When I started this spiritual journey, I had no idea then that Brian was very spiritual. During my massage, I told him about Sheila working with Isa. Finally, he and his wife, Jenn, decided they would have a reading done for their cats. Little did we know at the time that we were all following a trail of Divine breadcrumbs. More on that later.

About 10 months after learning of Brian's connection to my past life, I finally learned the identity of my second child. I was out for Christmas dinner with my friend, Kathy, who referred me to Sheila when Isa had initially become sick. Kathy and I would meet up and get immersed in spiritual talk. On this occasion, I'd been telling her about this past life, speculating about who this other child was. In the middle of our discussion, everything slowed down and I began receiving intuition from the Universe that the other child was Sheila.

I was feeling shivers all over my body and things got amplified so much that when I looked at Kathy, all I could see was her one right eye. I could feel my eyes moving back and forth rhythmically as if they were downloading the information into my consciousness. Kathy interrupted me by saying, "Earth to Wanda." As our eyes connected, Kathy said to me, "Your daughter is Sheila. It's Sheila, isn't it? I know it's Sheila." We both got the information at the same time. It felt so surreal, but true.

I went to bed that night, feeling honored and grateful that all these people had joined me in this life to assist me.

I told Brian about what I'd learned and he went still. At first, I thought he wondered if I was crazy, but then it became obvious he was processing. He told me he'd had a meditation, that he and Sheila had been brother and sister in a past life. This was more confirmation.

When I told Sheila, she was dumbfounded. She confirmed that she and Brian both had felt a past life connection as brother and sister. Brian had confided in her months before that he felt as if he'd been her big brother, had looked out for her. Neither Sheila nor Brian had told this to me before.

When Sheila connected with my guides about it, they were smiling and happy. Sheila jokingly said, "Hi, mom," and we hugged. She said, "Of course, I wouldn't get that intuition because I would interfere. That makes a lot of sense."

Sheila had noticed that whenever she would connect to my husband, Norm, she would never get as strong a connection as anyone else. Every time she was supposed to meet him, it wouldn't happen. Finally, the last time she was scheduled to meet Norm, she had car trouble. When she asked if she was supposed to go, the Universe said, "No, don't go. You're not supposed to go". The reason was Norm. The Universe didn't allow Sheila to interfere with me getting the information in the timing that was required. From that time onward, Sheila was never blocked from connecting with Norm or seeing him.

How often do we meet someone and instantly feel as if we've known them our whole life? We may understand this connection on a physical level but we often miss the spiritual connection. We all have soul groups who incarnate together to assist in learning. These groups are linked from one life to another and come into each incarnation without the memory of their past lives to provide the canvas for that learning. Why would we remember? It's a little like cheating by reading the last chapter of a book before starting it.

I used to call my husband my soul mate. At the age of 14, I knew when I walked past him in the school hallway that I'd marry him. It was very surreal because I'd never seen this person in my entire life. One day I was in band class – I played the alto saxophone – when Norm walked into the room. He was returning his trombone. I asked a friend who he was, and she told me the details. He was two years older than me, a star athlete, an honor student (second in his class) and he played music. He was also a super nice guy. It turned out that Norm was in the school band. The following year, at the age of 15, I was also accepted into the school band. I was very shy and so was he, but my twin sister worked tirelessly to get us together that year.

Now I understand that anyone can be a soul mate, it's not just reserved for life partners. They are souls from within your soul group. Some can bring a positive experience, some a negative experience. Some souls have contracted in spirit to provide negative experience for the sake of your learning. Some of the worst people in our lives may be from our soul group and be our greatest teachers.

This is why forgiveness is essential for spiritual growth. Forgiveness is a gift to the self. I once heard a quote about lack of forgiveness – it's like drinking poison and hoping the other person will die. Lack of forgiveness only harms you, no one else. The negative emotions get stored in the cells and this creates disease. Forgiveness doesn't mean the other person is right. It just means that you've released the negative emotion from your body, mind and spirit.

Not only is forgiveness a gift to yourself, but chances are you've had a life where you've lived from the dark, rather than the light, to help other souls with their own growth. If we've lived past lives from shadow, done terrible things, and our spiritual goal is to find self-love, then we can't attain self-love if we avoid forgiveness. We must be able to forgive ourselves and others. Self-love is also about honoring our soul's journey.

Chapter 15
Divine Breadcrumbs

About one year into our work, Isa said that times were changing for me. He said by the time I moved into the new year, about five months away, my life would look very different than the previous year. He wanted me to look back on the year and acknowledge what I'd achieved. He said:

> It's not egotistical to have pride in the self. You need to honor yourself for what you've achieved because you've done a lot of work and you've come so far and there's been so much.

Sheila commented further that it's the ego that tells us we shouldn't be proud of ourselves. The ego thinks, "You shouldn't be proud, you're not good enough".

What Isa was referring to was twofold. I'd been following this spiritual journey, and yes, I should be proud of myself but we were also following Divine breadcrumbs, part of a much bigger plan than we could have realized.

Several times, Isa would drop breadcrumbs, saying he was excited because I had turned a corner and we were on a different path now. He mentioned that I had another big project coming that I would be involved in and he'd say, "It's good". Little did I know just how big this project was going to be.

About five months after I started this spiritual work, Brian and I decided to write a blog together on holistic health. When I mentioned it to Sheila, she tapped into Brian's energy and said he shouldn't be a real estate agent. Brian was both a massage therapist and a real estate agent. Sheila saw him running a holistic clinic. It didn't appear that he solely owned it, but he would have a vested interest in it. I told Brian what Sheila had said and he admitted that he'd wanted to do this, but it required too much financing.

Fast forward to May 2012 when I went to see Brian for a massage. During the session, he told me that Sheila had a client who owned a wellness clinic, and she needed to sell it. This client was looking for a real estate agent. Since Brian had become a client of Sheila's, she'd put this woman in contact with him. Brian went to see the clinic, but as he looked at it, he knew he wasn't supposed to sell the clinic, he was supposed to buy it.

As Brian was telling me what had happened, I recalled what Sheila had said six months before, and immediately got excited for Brian. Although he was eager, he didn't know how he could make it work. First, he was living in Toronto and this business was 70 kilometers away. It would require uprooting his life. Since both he and his wife enjoyed the city, it would be a hard transition. Furthermore, he didn't have the money to pay the asking price of this business. I got excited for him. I told him he had to make it work, it was his destiny.

A few days later, I happened to mention it to my husband in an off-handed comment. Norm had also been seeing Brian as his massage therapist. When I mentioned that Brian needed financial backing, Norm said, "Maybe we should invest with him." My jaw hit the floor. I immediately emailed Brian with the proposition and he replied, "I asked my guides and they started snickering." Confirmation. We all became business partners in October 2012 when we purchased the business.

Sheila was right. Brian wasn't supposed to be a real estate agent.

He was only supposed to be a real estate agent as a stepping stone to acquire the business, which he would run, but not as a sole owner.

Ironically, my husband had just secured a line of credit so we could purchase a second home in Arizona. It was his dream to have a place to golf in the winter months so investing in this business meant giving up his dream. I'd later learn that he selflessly gave it up because he thought I wanted to partner in the business. However, buying the business had never been on my radar, had never been my desire.

I've since learned that my husband is divinely guided even though he's not aware of it. The Universe brought him to the business in whatever way it could. If it meant feeding him information that I wanted to be part of the business, then so be it. In reality, it was his sub-specialty in a new field of medicine that would be brought to this new business. Without it, the business would never have survived and without Brian's excellent entrepreneurial skills, Norm's sub-specialty couldn't have been as successful as it was.

My skills in medical systems, business systems and organization, and computer software, as well as weight loss management would bridge it all together and assist in the transition. My roles would be many. I worked tirelessly trying to better our systems as part owner of a growing business, often to the point of exhaustion.

The Universe rewarded my husband for listening to his inner guidance and giving up his dream. Four months later, his good friend bought a home in Arizona and gave my husband an open invitation to stay there and golf whenever he wanted. The Universe works that way, where one door closes, another opens.

There were many challenges along the way, and much worthwhile learning. The spiritual and business growth was exponential for all of us. We each brought to the business what was needed. It seemed as if the three of us together would make a whole. It was like magic happened when we all came together, working as one. But when we didn't work together, everything fell apart. Each person brought their own strengths. Where one didn't excel, the other could take up the baton. Had I not been part of the business, I wouldn't have grown as much as I have.

There were many impactful lessons that I needed to work through for the betterment of my being for my soul lessons. We were following divine breadcrumbs. The Universe had set it up perfectly. It all started when a little dog got sick and went to an animal communicator. As Isa said:

> It was a lesson in the divineness of spirit. When we follow a path it always takes us to some place we may not necessarily see, but Spirit is always working to create for us.

The Universe pulled us all together, four souls from a past life family entwined; Norm, myself and Brian running a business with Sheila as the spiritual business advisor, providing guidance from the Universe. Add to that a little dog from another past life of mine entwined with Sheila and myself, assisting us on this journey by providing guidance to us through Sheila as well.

I'm not sure where all of this takes us as a business, but I know that if we follow the Divine breadcrumbs, it will be whatever it's meant to be.

Chapter 16
Physical is Not Reality

One day in July 2016, Isa was in pain. His penis was red and swollen and he seemed to be licking it excessively. He stopped eating for a couple of days. Thinking he might have a urinary tract infection, I took him to the holistic vet. The vet did a blood work-up on Isa and his BUN and creatinine levels came back high with no evidence of an infection. Something was wrong with his kidneys.

Dr. Haighaght gave Isa IV fluids every second day for a week, trying to support the kidneys, along with a regimen of homeopathics. During this time, Sheila was also giving Isa Reiki.

After a week, Sheila said that Isa's kidneys felt better than they had the week before. He was visibly improving, urinating better and starting to eat. He even had some spunk back. I was feeling confident that Isa's kidneys were back to good.

Dr. Haighaght did a repeat test and his creatinine was even higher, so high that he was concerned that Isa was in renal failure. He recommended that Isa see an internist the following day in Toronto. Something didn't feel right. I had an appointment scheduled with Sheila the following day so instead, I scheduled the appointment with the specialist two days later.

During the session with Sheila, Isa told her that he thinks he has polycystic kidney disease. I went numb with fear. I immediately recalled that my beloved cat died at 8 years of age from this congenital condition. Isa was 7 ½ at the time. The similarities couldn't be ignored.

Isa stated that he thought he could be healed, that he was already on his way to healing. My logical side said, "How? It's congenital and degenerative." Isa's reply was, "How do people die and come back?"

A moment later, Sheila stated, "I think you're supposed to be addressing whatever happened with your cat, working to release it because that seems to be where Isa wants to go."

I divulged the story of my cat, Squeaky. All my life, I had never been much of a cat person. My skating coach developed asthma from her cat and she was desperately looking for a home for Squeaky. She asked me if I would take her because Squeaky didn't like other cats, so she was finding it difficult to place her in another home. After some thought, I decided it would be a good idea to have a playmate for my dog.

As it turned out, Squeaky came to me, not my dog. She changed my life. She was a dog in a cat's body, so affectionate and sweet. She'd come sleep on the bed while I read, purring, rubbing her face on my book and kneading her paws on my chest. She'd greet me when I came home. She was the most social cat I had ever met. Squeaky was determined to make people happy. Even my father, who never took to cats, was carrying her around in his arms in displays of affection.

When Squeaky was only eight years old, I came home and saw yellow stuff coming out of her mouth. I knew something was terribly wrong. I picked her up around the flank area and she attacked me. I took her to an emergency clinic and she bit the vet so they had to put gloves on to do an exam. They diagnosed her with abscessed teeth, specifically stating they couldn't find a problem with her kidneys in response to my concerns about her flank pain. In my relief that the vet – the expert - said she was ok,

I set aside my underlying gut feeling that something was terribly wrong. The vet sent me home with a prescription for antibiotics and told me to make an appointment for Squeaky to get her teeth cleaned. I happily obliged.

The antibiotics provided no relief for Squeaky. She was there physically, but she wasn't there mentally. Her eyes were dark and distant. She was a stranger. The morning of her dental appointment, when I picked her up to go to the vet, she attacked my hand viciously. I still have the scars.

An hour after Squeaky's scheduled cleaning, I was leaving my Chiropractor's office when I saw my husband waiting for me in the parking lot. This couldn't be good. He told me that when they took Squeaky's blood work, her creatinine levels were off the chart. She was in renal failure. She had been septic; she didn't have abscessed teeth and we would need to put her down. I doubled over, howling in grief. She was only 8! How could this be happening?

We drove to the vet's office to meet with him. To make matters worse, the vet read the emergency notes, which stated that Squeaky had bit the vet. Consequently, they were going to send her off for rabies testing. My husband said, "Over my dead body you're going to cut her head off for testing!" An argument ensued. We stated that it was a provoked attacked as a result of being septic and that Squeaky had been up to date with her rabies shots. We were shocked by the insensitivity of this vet.

My husband called Public Health and explained the situation to them; a fully vaccinated cat, provoked to attack due to renal failure was not a threat to the vet's health. Public Health compromised with us, saying they would freeze Squeaky's body for a week and if the vet showed rabies symptoms, they would have to send her for testing.

I was racked with guilt. I felt as if I had done something to cause Squeaky's renal failure. I felt as if I didn't do enough to pick it up early. Back then, I knew very little about health and anatomy. I went back through her files, and noticed that her previous physical showed that her creatinine levels had been on the highest end of normal they could be - essentially high - and the vet never said a word about it.

My husband asked for an autopsy, for the simple reason that he wanted to know the cause so that I wouldn't beat myself up. It turned out that her renal failure was a congenital condition, which poor veterinary medicine failed to pick up.

I never got over the circumstances of her passing; the absolute agony she lived with, being septic from renal failure for 4 days before she was released from her living hell. I never got over my anger at the vets, who lacked empathy and compassion, who never even diagnosed her condition when the blood work showed something was amiss. I never got over my guilt that I had not done enough to love her. My dog, Misha, was difficult to live with. He was the alpha and he didn't like Squeaky. That made things difficult for her. I always promised Squeaky that I would make it up to her after Misha passed but that promise was forever broken.

Following my story, Sheila channeled Squeaky in spirit. Sheila stated:

> She doesn't feel like she was neglected. She feels like she was comfortable, and quite happy with the level of attention she got because she didn't want to be smothered. She liked attention when she wanted it, but not

when she didn't.

She says she was a product of poor breeding. There was too close a bloodline mated together. She feels that she had problems in her earlier stages of life. She had a lot more turmoil in her younger years, being on edge. Other animals were around her and quite a few people. She was high strung for a good portion of her younger years. It feels like she had three homes.

She says you were a place to hung out, breathe and have a reprieve to the end of her life. She was looking for that sense of comfortableness, being allowed to be who she was freely and she believes that you gave her that so she's thanking you. She was not able to be herself in those other places because she was very confined and controlled. Then she came to you and you weren't controlling so she was able to blossom and be who she needed to be. She wanted to be that for a little while before she crossed, to stand in who she was.

She says she was there to assist you in having more compassion and understanding of cats because you were quite rigid with your beliefs.

She seems quite content in spirit. She can't move from spirit until you come to terms with the concept of her passing. You need to release her from your own self-doubt.

A part of you still feels like you need to make it up to her so she's saying until you release that concept, until you have a conversation and let her go, she can't reincarnate. She also says that you need to learn not to take on what's not yours. That's just a part of it. If you were meant to, you would have known she was sick. If she wanted you to identify her sickness, she would have shown you.

She's says you need to talk with her and come to terms with what happened and she needs to be released. She almost feels jailed by your negative emotions because part of you is still searching for a way to rectify the situation. Do you need to go through it again in order to make yourself feel better? Do you need to know you will make the right decisions? And then can you let it go?

I knew there was a connection and it hit me that perhaps I – or the Universe - was manifesting kidney disease with Isa in order to make things right.

Sheila continued, stating:

She's waiting for you to forgive yourself. She says you don't need forgiveness from her because there was never an issue. She holds no animosity towards you, even for the fact that she's been sitting in waiting for 16 years to be released. It's part of the journey and learning that you contracted with one another, she says matter of fact. She can't reincarnate until you deal with this because you're tying her, holding her.

She's so comfortable within herself and you allowed that. That was what you were supposed to do. You weren't supposed to save her. That's not the role. You're confused as to what your role was in that scenario and what was the learning. She says when a being comes into a space where there's genetically corrupt genes, they do that on purpose. It's a means to an end and she's saying it was her choice, not yours, so don't claim it.

She gave the opportunity for the vet clinic to learn. Hopefully, he [the vet] took the opportunity, but whether he did or not, it's not her responsibility. She's quite content with how everything played out.

With that, Squeaky was gone. Sheila and I discussed my life lesson of second guessing myself and allowing somebody else to make choices on my behalf. As we discussed Isa's appointment, which was scheduled for the following day, Sheila said:

> I don't pick up the kidneys in distress. It feels more like the Squeaky issue. I wouldn't be surprised. Look at all the things that have happened to both you and Isa that are beyond the scope of medical understanding, that are more spiritually related.

I went home and meditated, connecting with Squeaky. I thanked her for coming to me and gave gratitude for our moments together. I thought of all the things about her that made me smile, then I gathered up all the trauma I'd stored for 16 years and released it.

The next day, my husband and I went to the Internist. I was confident that Isa would be healthy, although a small part of me was nervous, naturally. The internist was already discussing diet, medication, and gloom, but when he returned from doing Isa's ultrasound, he looked perplexed. Isa's kidneys were normal. I asked how that could happen and the only explanation he could give us was that some dogs have naturally high creatinine levels. Of course, as I snickered internally, I knew that wasn't the case. A re-test of Isa's creatinine levels a few weeks later revealed his levels to be back to normal.

This was such an impactful lesson for me. What we see is not necessarily reality. The universe can work in incredibly mysterious ways, manipulating events for our learning. My whole life, I've been so logical, so grounded in the physical. This lesson helped me to understand that it's only one aspect of our reality. We aren't just a bunch of cells and DNA, we are so much more. When we believe in only what we can see, we potentially limit ourselves to a narrow existence and we miss the lessons. When we can see beyond that limitation, the outcomes are limitless. This is where supernatural healing can occur. This is where the true power lies.

I later asked Sheila if Squeaky was able to move on. Sheila tapped into her and said, "Oh my gosh, she's so happy. I just feel her frolicking and she feels unbound now. She's free, very happy and playful."

Part III
Speaking to the People

Chapter 1

About a year into our work, as I became more focused on the business, Isa said he felt like he had no purpose. The impression that Sheila received was that of someone retiring from their job. That made sense because his job had been to assist me. As I grew and transformed, he wasn't as consumed with his job. I still had a lot to learn, but I was listening and growing. His purpose was in transition. He had shifted from helping me heal on a personal level to a much larger scale, assisting me with lessons regarding the new business on top of my own personal lessons.

He said, "One day I would like to record a message to the people". It was just a seed being planted. About two months later, Isa brought it up again. He said he wanted to write a book. He wanted a platform for his voice.

Between the three of us - Sheila, Isa and I - we hatched a plan to start a blog. Isa would provide the material, Sheila would channel it, and then I would polish it up and post it on his blog, complete with pictures. I set up his blog on WordPress called Isa's Corner and Sheila provided a link through her website to promote his blog posts through her business Facebook page.

As the plan developed, Isa commented that, "It's about time we got here. I've been waiting." On December 5, 2012, we posted Isa's first blog. The following month he asked for a Facebook page so we could link Facebook to his blog posts. This was a good decision. Sheila shared Isa's words of wisdom on her own Facebook page and as time went on, he'd often have close to 900 views on his blog.

Isa wrote many types of blog posts, mostly words of wisdom. His very first blog was about how we choose to walk the path of our life, whether we stop to smell the roses or race through life without paying attention. Isa wrote a blog about the significance of a rainbow and how he'd like to be remembered as a rainbow after he passes. He wrote about how society shouldn't give its power to one person to rule us. Isa also blogged about life being like a game of tennis where we either play nice or not so nice. He wrote a blog about the essence of time and how we aren't present in the moment. He talked about how we should celebrate our life and to honor it every day, not just on birthdays. He talked about how we should rest and rejuvenate. Isa wrote about the importance of mankind working together, that we can't build a bridge alone. These were just a few of his early blogs; many will be shared in the next part of the book.

Isa blogged on meditations like consciously hydrating the body, a spring awakening meditation, a meditation to connect with the sun, and a meditation to honor the Earth.

Mostly Isa's messages were about self-love and honoring the self. It amazed me how much wisdom could come from a 5-year old dog. This type of wisdom wasn't from the physical world. How could a 5-year-old dog know so much? He knew about the human experience, the animal experience and a universal experience most humans have never had the opportunity or openness to access in a lifetime.

About four months into giving his spiritual messages, Isa decided that he'd like to do personal readings through his Facebook page. People could post a question to him on Facebook, and during our weekly session with Sheila, he'd give them his message.

Eventually, Isa stopped doing personal readings through his blog.

It was a difficult process as we didn't have the time to focus on other people's issues within my own sessions. It also lacked connection from the individual he was reading since they weren't in his presence. He did 16 readings, but eventually, Isa found another venue; group events. Although he continued with the blog posts, posting his words of wisdom, the group events would prove a better venue for connecting to people on a personal level.

Chapter 2
A Lesson in Animal Communication

Five months after starting his blog, one of Sheila's clients asked her to teach animal communication at her equestrian center. Sheila's client, Tricia, had been following Isa's blog so she asked Sheila if Isa would like to participate in the training as a demo animal to assist the students in communication.

Isa said he would like to go, but not as a demo animal. Instead, he wanted to give each of them a reading before their training started.

The day came. As everyone sat in the circle, I watched in amazement as Isa systematically connected to everyone, unbeknownst to them. I noticed that he was transfixed on one person at a time. I could tell from his eyes, dark and piercing, that he was reading them ahead of time.

The session started and Sheila explained to everyone how animal communication works, that she translates feelings, pictures and words that come into her head and assembles them together, almost like a puzzle. Sheila connected with Isa and began the process of Isa's first public appearance bringing spiritual messages to the people.

Isa chose Faye to read first. If anyone had doubts, they were quickly dismissed when Sheila communicated that Isa would like to go to her. I set Isa down and he darted to Faye, licking her face and feeding her energy as he did so. Isa told her that:

Your purpose is self-discovery, to go within and learn

who you are. You have gathered other people's beliefs over your lifetime, taking them in and storing them. You often push others to get to a space because you are so concerned for their well-being. But it's for you, not for them.

Pay attention to what that being needs, and do that if you're going to assist, but recognize that you don't need to. It's an option, not a requirement.

Then Isa checked in to make sure everyone in the room understood this concept. It wasn't just for Faye; it was for everyone. Isa continued, saying:

As humans, we try to fix instead of allowing. Maybe we see what would help someone, and if we push them in that direction, we know their problem would be solved. But maybe that person doesn't want to go that direction? Maybe they aren't ready? It's not your job to force them in that direction. Give them what they need, not what you require of them. Sometimes someone just needs a hug or flowers.

Faye commented on Isa's intensity as if he were gazing into her soul. Isa replied that:

That's what I want you to do, to gaze into yourself. It's vulnerable, and when it feels vulnerable, that's exactly where you need to go. You won't be disappointed in what you find because you have a beautiful soul. Don't be afraid to go there.

Isa's reading brought tears to Faye's eyes. She was so connected to Isa that he had to ask her to stop looking at him. He was so full of love for her that he was unable to disconnect to read the other people.

For the second reading, Isa chose Tricia. He asked to lie beside her and averted his gaze away from her during the entire reading. He said to Tricia:

> I want to respect your energy [by averting my gaze] because it is the only way accepting to you. I want to send love with respect because you don't receive love well. You are guarded about sharing openly who you are and it was conditioned in you so you need to learn that it's okay to express yourself.
>
> Don't worry about the judgments of others because their perception means nothing. It doesn't mean you don't love that person if you don't accept their judgments, it means you can love without taking those judgments on.

Isa also commented that:

> Every being has their own mission. When you see something occur, recognize that it needs to take place and don't feel sorrow. Instead, feed it positive. Know that you might not have to get why every little thing occurs, just accept and allow because you aren't meant to understand everything. Your job is to hold the light, to be the flashlight and allow your light to be.

The next person Isa chose was Nancy, the owner of a private horse boarding facility. He told her that:

> Your heart bleeds for animals and you place them above yourself. This is unsafe for you and it has cultivated

health issues within your body from sacrificing yourself. This saddens the animals that you would place yourself beneath them because that's not what they want. Their true wish is for you to love and respect yourself, then give love and respect to them. You need to shift your perception of how you're giving to the animals at the cost of yourself.

You don't notice it in one day, but over time you are personally deteriorating. Every time you sacrifice yourself for the animals, a piece of you gets destroyed. Rather, start with you, then aid the animals because you're crippling yourself and that's exactly what will happen to you if you don't change. If you don't change, in about 1½ years, you won't be able to walk.

Nancy replied that she'd told her husband the previous week that she's giving it two more years with the animals, and then she's done.

Isa added that:

This is a pattern you've created in your life, starting with the animals and spreading to your family and friends. Some of the animals, family, and friends manipulate you because their souls are trying to teach you about the concept of boundaries and limitations.

During the next two readings, Isa was panting loudly. He was thirsty and started to vomit. He wasn't handling the energy in the room well. Eventually, I had to take Isa outside because he had diarrhea.

For the last couple of readings, we had to take the group outside to a picnic table. Isa told the next participant, Susan, how she battles her negative thoughts, something she'd been trying to reverse from her conditioned upbringing. Isa wanted to reassure her that it's a long journey but not to give up. He encouraged her that, "It will get easier as you go along and the work will be well worth it."

Isa added that, "You have never felt understood in life and people misinterpret what you are about." Susan replied that it was all true, that Isa was the second one to tell her this, adding that she doesn't even remember her upbringing.

Isa told Susan to be careful of her right ear, that there's something going on with it. He added that:

> If it hasn't shown up yet, it will, so get medical attention when you notice. It feels like a swelling so you might feel some vertigo issues or discomfort when it presents itself. You also have a big sensitivity to molds so watch that and make sure you don't eat or drink anything that's mold or fungus-related, like mushrooms, wine, fermented foods, and dairy.

Susan commented that she'd cut out dairy, and she'd had a bad reaction to mushroom soup. Three weeks ago, she'd had horrible vertigo that kept her bed bound an entire day.

Isa commented that:

> People will never come to you. You will always have to go to them. Reach out because there are several layers of learning in that. You have to set the lead of the exchange in both your work and your personal life.

Your work is very important because you help people. Do not search outside your work for your purpose. It's what you do within the work that is your purpose.

The last person in the group was Kellie. Because Isa was so unwell, he did her reading a few days later during a session with Sheila. Isa told her that:

> Freedom is very important to you and the concept of freedom is what you have selected as a mission in this life. As a result, you will do a lot of things in your life that are somewhat rebellious but not in a negative way. Rather, you will try to find yourself and push yourself in order to feel like you're free, meaning independent of others. You don't like anyone to tell you that you are not allowed to do something or that you have to do something a certain way and this is the reason why. You don't like anyone trying to control you. You thrive on challenges so if someone says you can't do something it's how you motivate yourself to move forward.
>
> You had a past life as a male black slave and so that past life is prevalent in this life. He worked in fields that were hard to clear and you were forced to plant crops. However, the crops didn't grow very well because the soil wasn't very good so you and the other slaves were constantly getting in trouble for the crops not growing properly, even though it wasn't your fault. As a result, there are many issues around this past life and you've carried them forward into this life to try to help clear them. You will be on a mission for freedom and independence as well as clearing those other issues that are connected to the emotions felt in that past life.

Studying homeopathy or herbs would be good; not raw herbs, but putting herbs into a tincture would be good for you to get into because it will help you later on. You are going to come against stumbling blocks because the work that you're going to do in assisting others working with animals will only be able to assist you so far, then you will be blocked by the issue of physical ailments. That will become an issue so you will have to find a way to either educate yourself or have someone who works closely with you who can work to assist with physical ailments. This is something you need to focus on now.

I think you have lovely energy. There's a lot of beauty in your energy, but you are very fearful about being rejected. When you come to terms with the fact that you are a beautiful soul and that you don't need acceptance from anyone else, when you find your freedom and independence, then you will feel entirely different.

You will go through a transformation of about three to five years where you are really on a mission to build and discover yourself more so than ever before. Over those years, you will learn incredible things about yourself. Harness it and recognize that this is a good thing, that it will make you a better person.

In about five years, you will have your own facility where you are training and assisting other people. You will have to work really hard at being patient and nonjudgmental and understanding other people's requirements. You need to recognize that it's not about you, it's about them. If you teach from a place of it being about them, then you will be an excellent teacher. Your stumbling block is if you become self-conscious then you won't teach well.

I love you and thank you for taking care of [your dog], Max. Max feels like he's indebted to you for the care and concern that you provide him. You're like a lifeline but he is your lifeline. It goes both ways, not one way. You need him as a lifeline so it's made him feel very purposeful in his life. However, there will come a time over the next couple of years where his health is going to decline and he will need to exit and he will need your permission to go. That will be very difficult for you, but he wants you to remember that his love will be eternal, just as your love for him will be eternal and that you will meet again, so you should not be sad. You should rejoice in the beauty of the time that you've had together because it's a gift and Max's passing will be a gift as well. It's not for a while but I don't know if I'll be able to speak with you again so I want to give you that message on behalf of Max. He's saying thank you.

Kellie commented that Isa's reading was very accurate and thanked him.

Then Isa was finished. One of the ladies told him that he'd earned everyone's gratitude. The whole session was amazing despite Isa's difficulty releasing the energy. Just when I thought we were done, I watched Isa get up on the picnic table and bid farewell to each and every person. He made his way systematically around the table, not skipping a single person. He was methodical in his farewell, giving love as well as receiving it from each person. If you know anything about dogs, you'll know this is not dog-like behavior. Sheila would later tell me that Isa was humble, thanking them for sharing with him.

I remember driving home after that event, feeling that I had been part of something very big. I'd been going to my weekly appointments with Sheila and Isa, and I think I'd become immune to the little miracles that I experienced each week. I hadn't realized just how profound it all was. My eyes watered in gratitude as I drove home.

It took Isa the day to recover. He was ill and couldn't eat, hiding under his couch, where he wanted to be left alone. It took a lot from him and a lot from Sheila. However, based on his past history, I was somewhat shocked to see that by the following day, he had fully recovered.

Sheila remarked the following week that:

> Animal communication with Isa at that level challenges me because he takes me ten steps deeper. It requires even more focus and when he's talking, it's like the whole room disappears, that's how focused I have to become. I found it very tiring to do myself and then teach afterwards. I had less patience because I had hit this deeper spiritual level with him and then I had to come back and teach people in the physical. That was very difficult. I had to hold the space for him so I had to hold the energy for both of us.

Sheila saw the benefit because she remarked that, "I have to use that to bring my level of animal communication to a new level."

Isa summarized the event, saying that:

> I'd like to do that again but we all learned that what I envisioned it to be and what it ended up being were

two different things.

I liked that all the women were open and receptive but I'd like for them to know that I said those things from my heart for their betterment and if they would like to show their appreciation for me, then just acting on what I said to them would be the gift that they could give me. That would be the validation I would need to move forward and do this for other people. These women are the pioneers for my work and if they act on my advice and direction, I will know. Energetically, it will help me move on and I'll want to give that to other people. I'll be sitting back and waiting for them and their reaction to the whole situation.

People have to remember that surface love is one thing, but spiritual love is something entirely different. That connection we all created that day should be the basis, their guideline for living from love in this world. The way they opened and received me and my energy and my love is the way they should open and give love to others.

Every time I communicate with somebody in this way, it's like a seed I plant, an attunement I create. They're like a link so now their chain is linked to that energy and then they can send it out and gift it to others and then the more links we create, the stronger the chain gets, the more powerful the energy.

I would like them to know that I had fun. I don't want them to pity me or feel bad. I'm fine. I recognized, with their assistance, my own requirements and limits and I'm grateful for that so it's very important that they don't feel bad for me, otherwise it taints what I'm doing.

It was a process just like we all go through and I'm better because of it. Animals don't want pity and when we pity the animals, we weaken them. And that goes for people too. Even though animals recognize that it weakens them, people do not. People grasp it and think that it's a good place to be. Animals realize it's not. They don't want to be there. When you pity an animal, you do a disservice to it.

Isa thanked me for taking him and sacrificing my own time for his needs and those of the other people there. Without me, he knew it wouldn't have happened. He thanked Sheila as well because without her there would be no message.

Isa told Sheila that they'd both have to learn how to do animal communication for bigger crowds and maybe send a global message instead of individual ones with 2-minute readings for a few people. He added that we need to take animal communication to a new level, filling auditoriums where the three of us sit up front and he would sit on my lap in order to anchor his energy because he's comfortable with me. Then Sheila would translate. He said we need to start smaller but aim for big events, like an auditorium of 300-500 people. He wanted to plan his first event for the fall of 2013 and wanted it videotaped so that we could share it on YouTube. Then he asked for a business meeting to discuss logistics.

It was all quite hilarious when you think of a little dog asking for a business meeting. I had visions of Isa attending the meeting wearing a tie and carrying a briefcase but nothing in my life has been normal since 2011. It completely freaked Sheila out, but we were being asked to trust.

Isa apologized to me that it's not about me anymore because we're shifting. He didn't want me to feel bad. Although I had expressed being ecstatic by this shift in so many ways, he wanted to verbalize it for my human side. From my perception, my human was happy because when I'm happy he's healthy and then he can focus on other things. If he's focusing on me, it means that I'm not doing well.

Isa said that we're all shifting together. He added that we've come together as a family and we will shift united, we will shift jointly. I was close to tears; my heart had opened so wide. Then Isa went on to say that:

> Our soul circle had planned this. This is the moment of truth and the moment of glory coming. I won't let you down. Our soul group had plotted this "attack" on humanity and I won't let anybody down, my link will be strong.

There was more drive in this little 7-pound dog than I've seen in most humans. Despite never feeling 100%, he just continues to move forward, doing what he came here to do, fulfilling his soul purpose - to bring spiritual messages to people from a canine perspective. We could all learn from him.

Chapter 3
Feedback

I followed up with all the women in the animal communication course to see how things had developed in their lives since Isa's reading. Interestingly, the ones that replied all knew each another so their stories intertwined.

The first person to reply to me was Nancy. She said:

> We have used Sheila on more than one occasion and have been comforted by our experiences and insight. I think it's truly wonderful to know what animals have to tell us. Last year, just before my mother passed, we received a message from Kellie's dog "Max" who was in Florida at the time. Max had a close bond with my mother and used to visit her in the nursing home and sit on her lap when she was still living with us. Max had started circling, wetting in the house and crying non-stop so Tricia and Kellie contacted their communicator [Sheila] to find out what was wrong.
>
> They called me to explain why my mother was hanging on for nine days without food or water or oxygen. She had been blind since she was seventeen and started to pass on but was enjoying "seeing" everything and everyone for the first time. She wasn't quite ready to go. After hearing what this little dog told me, it helped me to assist her crossing over on the tenth day. I get goose bumps every time I think about it. I think animal communication is extremely important and uplifting. I can't say enough about it!

I smile when I think of Isa's reading for me. He said I was pretty and that made me smile. It is interesting that Isa spoke about me getting sick. In October 2014, I fell through the haymow in my barn and broke my back, shoulder and pelvis, forcing me to slow down in a big way. It was human error and I was rushing to do something for the horses. It was raining and I was wearing the wrong boots. I had to relinquish chores and the control of my barn. It was monumental for me. I blew a vertebra and compressed another so I am 3 inches shorter as well, which is a constant reminder.

My husband retired last January to help run the business and it was the best thing he could have done. Everything has worked out in a way I never thought possible. Isa probably already knows that! LOL. Last April, I was able to go back to the barn part time and now I am back fully. Last week I was finally able to get on a horse again with no pain, something I used to take for granted. I guess the journey is the thing!

Tricia, author of the book, "Summer's Garden Gratitude in Nature", was next to reply, and this is what she wrote:

In 2010, I found myself in a situation where I was transporting my two horses from the Caribbean to Ontario. Although the trip was well organized it was still stressful. They flew from the Island where they lived to Miami. Upon my arrival there, I was notified that they would need to be quarantined for approximately four weeks as a result of a paperwork issue between the US and Canada at the time. I was very concerned.

I was aware that people claimed to be able to talk to

animals but I hadn't yet met any. As the days went by, I couldn't stop thinking about my horses alone in quarantine in a strange place so I turned to the internet and found an animal communicator in Florida who agreed to help me. Leading up to the call with her, I was filled with mixed emotions from nervousness to skepticism but mostly excitement. In short, the call was wonderful! I could feel and hear that the communicator was indeed talking to my horses. I was able to tell them that they were not abandoned but in transition and soon would be with me in their new home. It was such a relief to hear from them that they were okay and now understood what was happening. I was hooked! I felt like dreams really do come true.

After they arrived and settled in, I shared my story with the barn manager/owner who told me about Sheila so we arranged to have her come out one evening so we could meet and she could do some readings. It was a wonderful event and soon we booked more visits and a couple of workshops.

Not only can Sheila talk to our animal friends, but she also shares her knowledge and supports those who have an interest in learning how to talk to animals themselves. Sheila teaches that it is actually a reawakening of connections we are born with.

During one of these workshops Sheila brought along two special guests, Isa and his mom, Wanda. We had heard about Isa and were all curious to meet him. It was a real privilege to spend that day with Isa and Wanda. When we met Isa, it was obvious that he is very much a dog who was fascinated with my cat and all things that dogs are fascinated with.

When it was time for Isa to share with us he became totally focused on the students as he talked to them one at a time with Sheila's assistance. The first thing I noticed was his eye contact that was filled with warmth and unconditional love. Although the information he shared was specific to the person he was focused on, there were common themes. These themes included that we are all connected and it is time for humans and animals to live in harmony with themselves, others, animals, nature and the whole planet and Isa is here to show us how. I heard Isa talk about this message again during two public forms.

Since then, I am doing my best to live this connection and be in harmony with all life. This is a process but one that is very important for today's world and during the process there are many, many rewards along the way.

I for one can feel Isa's support, for his heart reaches far and wide! He may look like a Pomeranian but his love is connected to the love energy that connects us all. This experience has changed my life in many ways and continues to do so!

Kellie replied that:

This reading resonates more now than it did at the time it was initially given to me. I can now see that I am on a journey to finding freedom, financial freedom, freedom to schedule and plan on my own terms, freedom to do what I want with life. I don't subscribe to the typical ways of doing things which is what I think he means by me being rebellious. If I want something, I find a way. I don't necessarily wait until the timing or the finances etc. are lined up.

I think I am just starting to get into learning about energetic ways of clearing physical ailments. It is true, mental, emotional and spiritual aspects are all important, but we cannot deny the physical and I have learned more about the others in the past and am playing some catch up to learn more about the physical, though it is all very complicated!!

The facility part is true! And so exciting. I can't wait to be into my own place and teaching out of there. I think I have done a good job recently of not being self-conscious about my teaching and just giving to students what I think they need, not worrying about what they will think. I have found this to be successful so far!

Max is still with me, lying beside me as I type. I am not sure when he will transition as his zest for life is as strong as ever. He still loves to play and eat and be loud and silly, but I can see that his body is becoming tired. I have given him my permission to pass when he is ready, but to stay as long as he wants!

Shortly after Isa's reading, Susan sent feedback to Isa's Facebook page. She said:

Thank you again for my personal reading you did in a group session back in May. You had a challenging day with so many people but all went well!

I had an ear problem which you mentioned and all is well now. I listen to my reading often and continue to act on your messages. Many thanks.

I provided this feedback so you can see how Isa's messages affected the lives of the women from the group. It's clear that he impacted them in a way that bettered their lives.

Chapter 4
Group Events

Following the animal communication event, Isa shifted. He started to blog a little differently. He blogged about his soul purpose and what he came here to do.

Isa said:

> This blog is preparation for what I am beginning to cultivate. It's my mission in life to bring information to people and I elected to come in as an animal because animals have limitless intuitive abilities and limitless access to dimensions and psychic information. They have a constraint in their physical body that limits them from being physically advanced. However, humans have a more physically diverse ability but have more limited spiritual intuitive abilities.

> Humans will begin to recognize this over the next 50 years and as a result, this will become more accepted. Eventually the way that we do life will be shifted. People will look to the counsel of the animals on a more conscious level to assist them in improving the earth and understanding globally what needs to be done to make the earth more viable, making less of a negative impact on the earth.

> People are going to become more green-conscious. Going forward over time there are going to be some shifts in our resources and people will go back to a more "green" way, a more basic way of providing life for themselves and sustaining themselves. People will

look to the animals to guide them in what resources are healthy and how they can change and we will begin to see buildings and structures being taken down and a replanting of the forest. Homes will be built into the land rather than killing the land so houses will be built within the forest around the vegetation.

I've selected to come here in the shape and form of a dog but I chose to do that because I wanted the higher spiritual connection and the greater awareness to "all that is" so that I could educate others. As I mentioned, if I had incarnated as a human this time around, I would have been limited. I might have had more physical access to things but I would be limited by my vibrational frequency so I elected to become a dog. And in this case, I am now electing to teach people this new way of being. In this way, I feel that I'm going to impact things on a greater scale. I wish for the opportunity to speak to groups of people, to educate them on what I have access to, what I can tap into. And I will call to myself groups of people to come and hear me speak and I will provide them with information based on the needs of the group as a whole. I will not know what I'm going to actually speak about until a couple of days before I present in front of the group. I'll start to be able to formulate it beforehand. I will have an understanding but it will come out in the moment depending on which people elect to be present in the group to hear my messages. Because of my connection to spirit and the understanding of spirituality, I am excited and honored, grateful to be able to present that to people. My mission is to help people by educating them in this way.

I feel relieved when people hear me. I love people and

this is why I've selected to do this. Because of love.

As we began initial preparations for Isa's event, he said:

> Thank you, mommy, for helping me because I couldn't
> do this without you. Do you see now why it was so
> important for you to stop blocking yourself and open to
> what was available? It goes far beyond you.

I realized I was blocking his destiny. What would have happened that fateful day had I chosen to walk away from what the Universe and Isa had asked of me? This was so far beyond me that I became emotional.

Isa said that:

> It's not a mistake that you resisted and blocked so
> don't feel guilty. You had to find the way here and you
> wouldn't have found it without blocking.
>
> Do not hold guilt or anything negative because now that
> you can see it, wasn't it a beautiful creation? Your story
> is far more rewarding because of the difficulty you had
> to endure than if it had been an easily-travelled road.
> People will have more connection with you and you'll
> have more impact when you share your journey and
> the struggles you went through and where you've come
> from. You're going to be an inspiration for many.

Isa said, "We have found our mission." Sheila said that he showed us like a triangle, a trinity, that we had planned this in spirit. Isa mentioned that I need to research the Celtic trinity knot. After learning that it symbolized many trinities such as "body, mind, spirit" and "Father, Son, Holy Ghost" to name a few, I also learned that the circle within it represents spiritual unity with the divine, a connection that cannot be broken. That was the three of us; a connection that couldn't be broken.

Isa said to Sheila that:

> Even though you doubt and you're not fully in with both feet, I know in your heart, you know that this is the right journey. It's your physical being who can't jump in full force because it's not the way you handle things. I can't speak without your voice.

Sheila explained that Isa was lightheartedly laughing at her because it hits insecurities within her. He told her that she might have to give up some things she wants and enjoys in order to deliver the messages required. However, he said that none of this is a sacrifice, that it's all a gift.

Shortly after, we set the date for Isa's first group event for September 7, 2013. Isa outlined in his blog post what could be expected.

He said:

> It is from my heart with love that I express the following message to those who are called to come and hear my messages through the medium of Sheila.
>
> I am excited to be able to share my wisdom with you. I think that you will all be surprised as to the level of intellect and insight that a young dog can carry forward. It is my hope that these messages that I bring to you at my event will help you to see your own worth and help you tap into your own greatness, the greatness that you hold

within, so that you can understand that you are a superior being as well. We all have this within us and I would like to be a shining example of what we are able to experience and tap into should we choose to allow ourselves to accept them.

I can guarantee you that you will come and feel great love during this event. That will be my focus for this meeting, to channel love and help all to understand that this is the common thread that we all share. Love is something that we all yearn for, love is something that we all search for, love is something that we don't always feel deserving of, but it's something that is always present should we choose to accept it. Love is something that we can freely share. It's the one thing that doesn't cost anything in this world and it's one thing that we can openly and honestly give to another from our hearts that can assist another in the betterment of their own journey.

Although my messages won't be solely about love, love will be the thread that holds all my messages together for that day so if you choose to come to hear my messages you will be guaranteed to feel the love, Universal love, that we all have the ability to channel.

My space will be a safe, trusting, loving, sacred space for all who wish to come so please put your inhibitions aside and if you feel that you are called to come see me then I would be honored to have you come to share in this special day with me.

During the preparation for Isa's event, he was the driving force for the creative aspects of the group event, while we worked to carry out his wishes. Isa told us what kind of a logo he wanted.

This wasn't the first time he'd created a logo. He had assisted me in designing two other logos for my business and then I had them created by a graphic designer.

For his logo, I took pictures of his paw and then sent them to a graphic designer to carry out Isa's instructions. He selected a friend of Sheila's named Peter Wolf to do the professional graphics work. Peter is a talented shaman who could communicate with Isa, so he was able to design the logo to exactly what Isa envisioned. Isa also came up with the tag line around the logo, "Spiritual Messages from a Canine Perspective". It's the same logo used in this book.

Isa requested shirts with his logo on them too so Sheila and I would have an "outfit" to wear during the event. We laughed when he said he wanted "Translator" on the back of Sheila's shirt and "Staff" on the back of mine. He has such a sense of humor! Needless to say, those titles were conveniently left off the shirts. Isa also requested a bandana to wear with his logo on it.

Two days before the big day, Isa was anxious, wanting to make sure the video would be ready. He said that he'd like a YouTube channel to post the video. He then thanked me for all the work and sent love to both Sheila and myself. He said he couldn't have picked two better souls to work with. The energy that came through Sheila was so loving and beautiful that it was making her cry. He added that, "We're like the three musketeers; all for one and one for all" – the trinity again.

Chapter 5
The Big Day

September 7, 2013 finally came. There were about 25 people at the event, which pleased us all.

Unfortunately, the videotape we wanted to post to YouTube didn't record the sound so we were unable to provide specific details of the event. Isa knew all along that there would be problems with the recording.

Aside from technical difficulties, the event was a huge success. It started out by me giving a heart-felt synopsis of the journey that Isa had led me through over the previous two years; a journey that had transformed my life. This was delivered with so much love for what Isa did for me that it was difficult at times to speak. I could clearly see from other people's reactions that they were also affected. There was hardly a dry eye in the house.

Isa thanked me and then went to work through Sheila. But first Sheila explained to the audience how animal communication worked.

As Isa began his spiritual work, he talked about the difference between compassion (love) and pity (feeling bad) whether it applied to animals or humans. To feel pity for someone is not to honor that soul's journey. Instead, we need to send that animal or human love in honor of what they have selected.

One astute guest later commented that it made her look back on my story about Isa and ask herself whether she had felt compassion or pity.

As Isa continued, he talked about the importance of touch and play. Then he jumped down and greeted all the guests, touching them and spending time with them. Just like the animal communication event, Isa methodically made his way around the room, greeting everyone until he ended back at front stage.

****

Following intermission, Isa did personal readings, providing almost everyone there with some insight.

Isa had a special message for a young female participant named Jess, but he didn't want to put the spotlight on her. After the event, he answered her burning question, whether she should see her father. Isa replied:

> It's difficult when we look at adults or people who are elders to us, who are supposed to be more knowledgeable, more sensitive, more aware and more understanding. It's difficult to look at them and know that and see through them and realize that they don't match our expectations.
>
> You need to be very aware that every being has their own lesson, their own journey. They grow at their own speed and in their own time and we have to honor that, no matter if that's our mother, father, child, brother, sister, or pet. We have to honor everything that soul decides to go through.
>
> You will come across many times in your life where you will see beings that don't have the same intellect, viewpoint, compassion and understanding as you do. So, learn this now, learn not to condemn them for not being in the same place you are. Instead, hold compassion for them and ask yourself, "How can I help them get beyond

where they are?" You're very lucky that you are beyond where they are. You've already learned so it's not their fault that they haven't. It's just like you would not want anyone to condemn you for not being educated in something.

It's very important that you step back. I would suggest that you take at least two weeks to evaluate and gather your thoughts, looking at him in a new light. Instead of looking at him for what you wish him to be, look at him for where he is as a soul and honor his journey. Don't focus on the disappointment you hold for what he hasn't done for you, he's simply incapable of that. When you recognize that he is incapable, hopefully you will understand that your expectations of him are unrealistic. This is just a fact.

Recognize that it's not about anything you've done wrong, it's only about where his soul chooses to be and what he's chosen to learn. At the same time, you don't want to hurt yourself by being exposed to this energy when it doesn't feed you in a positive light. For this reason, I would suggest that you have a distant relationship with him after you come to terms with understanding where he's at and that it's not your fault. Have a distant relationship with him whether it be through electronic connections such as cell phone or email instead of a personal relationship with him.

Work to build yourself to a space where you feel comfortable, because there is an onus put on you to be responsible for your adult father that is not fair or realistic for you at your age. Sometimes others around you place expectations on you and you feel responsible and that's your personality. This is the lesson for you to begin to understand that when others place expectations on you, you have a choice to accept them, feeling accountable and responsible, or not. And in this case, I'd suggest you don't.

Learn to love yourself and learn to accept what's important to you. I'm not saying you should harm others by your choices, but if what you need is not to see him, then you can tell him or word it in a way that's not harmful. There is a lot of anger, frustration, aggression and disappointment in you that needs to be cleared in another way so I would also suggest that you go see someone outside of your family that you can talk to to help you release those energies. You don't need that emotion in you. It's just harming you.

I want to tell you that I love you very much and I see your beautiful heart and I see your beautiful light. Just because others don't see that within you, doesn't mean it doesn't exist so always remember that please. When I kiss you all over and get excited about you, it's because I feel your love and I'm so excited to exchange love with you because your heart is very innocent. I really worry because I don't want anybody to interfere with that innocence of your heart. You need that going forward.

When you grow older, you're going to help people who are not well and you will work in the medical field but not in the same way as your mother. You will help others so you don't want to lose the innocence of your heart because it's the innocence of your heart that feeds the love to others which is what your passion and purpose is on this Earth. You will help others feel good about themselves and you'll help them learn how to accept themselves no matter where they are in their journey, in their life, and no matter what anybody else thinks.

So, use that concept with your father and understand that he needs to learn to accept himself – and he doesn't – so his actions and words are more self-reflective than they are pointed at you. It's hard to watch somebody harm themselves but sometimes you just have to accept it and feed them love anyways.

The readings were followed with a question and answer period. One of the guests asked if Isa was typical of all animals. Sheila responded that all animals have the ability to communicate, but she'd never communicated with an animal so advanced as Isa.

To end the event, Isa had us all connect our energies to one another through a group meditation, then send love out to the world.

It was a relief that Isa had learned to manage the energies in the group better than his first group event.

Chapter 6
Isa's 2nd Event

Isa's second event took place on February 2, 2014, the day after his fifth birthday. Due to persistent health issues, the size of the event was limited to 15 people to allow Isa to manage the energies.

This time the event recorded, so we were able post his video on his blog.

Isa chose to discuss the freedom to live and why we incarnate. Through Sheila, he said:

> At this time, universally, we are all feeling a great shift and change so a lot of you are feeling somewhat confused as to why you've come to partake in the life you have chosen, why you're living, depending on your understanding of incarnation and what your core beliefs are.
>
> Last year was the beginning of this transition of shedding the old and stepping into the new, so as we move into 2014, we are all experiencing shifts in the understanding of why we have come here, what is our meaning, what is our purpose, and what are we meant to do? It's like reawakening and restarting your life so many people will have experienced that over the last little while and will be facing that now. There will be huge shifts in your lives and a huge desire to alter your life into something new.

Going to the concept of when we're in spirit, we are all made up of the same thing, whether an animal, a person, a tree or a blade of grass. We are all energy. We all start as energy and it is just the choice that we make as to what we choose to create from that energy, what illusion we choose to provide for others to see. Meaning, do we choose to take the form of a person or the form of an animal or take the form of a plant? Those are all choices that we all have, so before we incarnate, we select what energy form we would like to take.

While in spirit, you have selected this, so recognize that being human was your choice. Often people look at animals and think, "Next time I come back, I'm coming back as a dog or a horse etc.," but don't forget that you selected the shell, the form, that you're in for a reason. Instead of wishing you were something that you're not, why not make the best of what you are? It's important on that note, to honor what you've selected because your soul was very wise in choosing what it wanted. Don't forget that your soul selected who you have chosen to be and it's very important that you honor yourselves because of that. Don't wish you're something that you're not, because if you wish you're something that you're not, then you dishonor your self and your selection.

Isa asked each person in the audience to:

Take a moment in your minds and tell yourself that you're grateful that you selected the form that you have because you did it for a reason. You may not always understand in this moment, but your soul selected the vehicle that you have for specific reasons.

Which leads me to my next point - the reason why you choose to incarnate. You select the vehicle first, then secondly, you decide how your life is going to be played out. You previously selected what you want to learn in your life, then you select your vehicle, then you select how your life is going to play out based on the vehicle you've selected. Everyone selects their own learning, their own understanding and then manipulate their life based on the shell they have chosen. Many of us choose difficult lessons and we also choose not-so-difficult lessons. We don't always notice those because they don't stand out so much because they're easy to walk through. The difficult lessons are the ones we tend to pay close attention to because our being feels them to the most emotional depth.

When we are in spirit form, we all hold a specific vibration and it is the accumulation of our lives that create our vibrational frequency. As a spirit you are light and a vibrational frequency. That vibrational frequency is set at a certain level and as you incarnate and learn the lessons and experience the positive and the negatives, it transforms you and amplifies your vibrational frequency each and every lifetime, depending on how many lessons you select.

As you learn your lessons, you increase your vibrational frequency. The whole point of incarnating is to learn and experience. Sometimes we as a spirit elect to increase our vibrational frequency only a small amount, so the lessons are not as extravagant or not as plentiful in one lifetime as they are in another, but it doesn't mean that it's a less "meaningful" life, it just means that it's what you selected, it just is.

When you incarnate and you walk through the lessons, the key to understanding your lessons is that you've forgotten what they are. You know the playbook, you know what you're getting into beforehand, and you come through as a soul very enthusiastically into your life. But as soon as you hit that change of form into human, you begin to forget what you had planned to do and why you had planned to come. Of course, it would make it simpler if we remembered and then we would fly through our life with less emotional turmoil but we wouldn't learn as much as we do when we forget. It's like going to take a test and knowing the answers for the test already. We wouldn't be challenged and therefore we wouldn't evolve. You only evolve when you learn through experience without the pre-knowledge of what you were supposed to be learning. So, we should honor all our experiences because they increase our vibrational frequency, they help us to evolve through life.

When we talk about experiences, most people go to negative experiences they've had, but I'd like you to recall a positive experience you've had that created growth as well. It's in the positive and the negative that we grow.

Those of us who've come to Earth at this specific time, to incarnate, have taken on a lot of challenges so that we could all grow more quickly. As the years have passed and souls have chosen to incarnate, the learning has become quicker and denser than before. Years ago, there was learning, but it was usually lifelong learning. There was one challenge and it took a lifetime to learn that lesson, but now everything is speeding up and we've begun learning faster and faster. This includes the planet as a whole, including the plants, the animals, etc. This is because as a soul species, we have elected to evolve faster. A molecule vibrating faster creates more energy, so as we vibrate faster, there is more light. This is what our souls are trying to do, vibrate quicker to become more light. And as we vibrate quicker, our vibration increases and we are more light. This is the concept of spiritual evolution.

The vehicle you've chosen to incarnate in is your soul's special tool to be able to process through the learning and you need to take really good care of this tool. The tool isn't disposable or recyclable like throwing it in the blue bin to make it into something else. Your body is all you've got for the time you've selected to be here and souls tend to forget that. The more you are in tune with your spiritual or soul vibrational frequency, the more you forget that you need this tool of the body. I am also guilty of this, which is why I am choosing to share it. I no longer need to be sick to the extent that I was to get my point through, but sometimes I get sick because I forget to take care of my body.

It's important to honor your shell, your vehicle, and make sure to commit that you will drink water. Humans are becoming less and less connected to the water sources and more and more fearful. When we ingest anything in fear, we are not feeding positive energy into our body. We are instilling fear into whatever we are ingesting. If you ingest water and it comes from a source that you believe to be unhealthy, and you ingest it anyways, then it will not help your body to the degree that it should. Find a way to believe that your water source is healthy for your body. If that means you have to change your water source, then please do. If it means you have to add something to your water, then do that. If you have to drink out of a special cup, then do that. Whatever you believe is what you will create in the body. The body is primarily made up of water so I'm talking about water because it's one of the most important substances you can put into your vehicle. If you want to run something, you have to put in the right source to make it run. For everyone, the primary source of fuel is water.

Let's understand why we come. We come to learn lessons and experience things, but it's not just about learning. Learning is always coupled with experience. If you don't have the experience, then there isn't any learning. When you understand something, it's not enough. You have to experience it. This is why we're given opportunities of exchange in our lives, why we have other souls who assist us in learning our lessons because we could learn for ourselves, but we can't experience without the interaction with others.

Turn to the person beside you and thank them because they are assisting you in learning through the act of experiencing. We're all linked in that way. We have all decided to assist one another so when you meet another person, whether they've cut you off in traffic or they're smiling at you in a lineup, understand they are all choices of interaction. As we choose to interact, we give the gift of assisting others in experiencing. Every time - whether it's positive or negative - that someone assists you, it's very important to honor them and thank them for participating in your journey, in your experience.

Earlier, my mom mentioned why I came - what was my

purpose - but I already knew my purpose. I just wanted her to understand my purpose. Sometimes we have to get crafty in order to assist ourselves and others in understanding what our role is and what their role is. In order for me to get her to understand what her role was, I had to express my role and get her to clearly understand my role, then she could understand her role and my experiences and what her purpose was as well. As I brought her to the space of understanding what my purpose is, I also brought her to the understanding of what her purpose is. We do that for each other all the time. If you pay attention to the people around you, even strangers, they will give you gifts, they will give you clues, as to what your purpose is.

No matter what we do in this life, we do not have to have notoriety to really impact the world. Notoriety is the basis of the ego, but the soul does not require the attention. It doesn't demand, "Look at me, look what I did." The ego does. What would we be without ego, though? We would just be souls and that would be boring because we've already been there [in spirit] and that's not why we're here. We are here to experience in a different form and a different life, a different confinement so that the experience becomes more profound. Therefore, we have the ego mixed in there to assist us in needing and acquiring things through emotion. Your soul technically does not need the notoriety but the ego does so when we talk about our purpose, why we are living, we can understand that first and foremost it's for learning and experiencing through action. And secondly, it's "What can we provide to others?"

Love is always the most important thing. How we live

and how we exchange with others always comes through love. Sometimes it is disguised in something that appears to be other than love, but I can guarantee that everything that occurs, every interaction that one has is always through soul love. Even someone who harms someone else in a negative way, comes from the basis of soul love. Soul love is different than what we understand as humans and animals in this day and age. Soul love is a higher vibration, is a higher accepting and it's an understanding that no matter what occurs, no matter what transpires, there is always an honoring at a soul level that goes far deeper than anything that we in our current form can understand.

I would like you to take a moment and take three big, deep breathes in and out. As you breathe, it channels the energy through the body and allows you to process the information that I just provided for you. In this moment, I would like to honor every one of you for coming today to participate in my learning and experience and through your action of being present today. You've assisted me in my learning and I hope that my being present today has assisted you in your action of learning. I thank you from my heart and I send you love.

I'd like everyone to close their eyes so you can be present in the moment and feel the energy that I'm going to send to you. [moment of silence]

When you're sitting, and wondering, "What is my life purpose?", you're all living it. That one purpose we look for, to say, "This is my destiny, this is my life purpose," is an illusion of the ego. Everyone's life purpose is simply in being and experiencing and you've all been doing that already. You've all experienced your life purpose already, the life purpose from a soul perspective. Sometimes your ego needs to have that one thing, that notoriety. So, create the illusion for yourself. What would you like that notoriety to be? What would you like that life purpose to be in that form? If you're not sure, then make it up. It's truly what it is - an illusion.

If you don't know, you don't need to go seek anybody out to find out your life purpose. You've already been living it, but your ego's purpose would be whatever you want it to be. If you believe it's to help children, then yes, that's your ego's purpose, that's your illusionary purpose. If it's to write, then yes, that's your purpose. If it's to create beautiful art for others to enjoy, then that's your purpose. If it's to facilitate the healing of others, then yes, that's your purpose. If it's to care for those who come before you or after you, then yes, that's your purpose. If it's to make the world a better place, to help rejuvenate the Earth, then thank goodness because we need more of that.

It's important that you all understand and realize – and I hope you've grasped my message today - that every single one of you is important. You are all important to anyone you encounter. You're important just because you've selected to be here. Choosing to incarnate is more difficult than choosing to stay in spirit so I honor you all and I honor myself for that difficult choice we've all made to come and be here and to experience in this way. The easy way out is to stay in spirit or go back to spirit, but the difficulty is standing here and participating in this way.

I want you to realize that each and every one of you are everything that you need to be. Each and every one of you are enough because you're already soul and you're already love and you've always been that. That's never changed. I find it ironic that so many people search for love but they're already love. Why are you looking for something that you already are? It's like trying to find your glasses when they're already on your face. It's the ego creating the illusion that you don't have love, so break through the illusion of the ego and accept the love that you already hold for the self.

We're moving into a time of the throat chakra, which is the energy center that governs communication, self-confidence and truth. You will all be experiencing primary lessons around those three things. When you do experience those lessons, stand back and identify them, then come from a place of love for the self and others when you experience them.

Life is a challenge, but life is also a gift.

Isa opened the floor to questions. The first question was for an explanation of ego. Sheila replied that:

The ego is a gift to the spirit that makes us human because without the ego we are still souls. The ego is the little voice inside of us that challenges everything. It can drive us forward, it can prevent us from doing something, but it is a vibrational frequency that constantly challenges the soul.

Isa added that:

The ego can be your best friend or it can be your worst enemy. Ego is everything that is not your soul and your soul is pure light, pure love, so everything else is ego. Ego is that nasty voice in your head that tells you that you can't do something. The soul says you can. The ego fills in the blanks to create a driving force for us to move forward. It's not necessarily a good or bad thing, it's just a complement to the soul to assist in achieving what is required.

Someone from the audience asked if the ego was something that should be suppressed or embraced? Isa replied that:

It depends on the circumstances. You need to keep the ego in check so it doesn't prevent you from doing what you need to do. It will challenge you and try to prevent you from learning and taking the action of learning. However, sometimes the ego will also motivate you to do exactly the same thing so the key is understanding yourself, knowing when the ego is present and how the ego is influencing you and then to harness the ego to complete whatever you require. Sometimes the ego can be fun because it feels good, but the key is to recognize when you're standing in the ego, and you harness it. You can have fun with it as long as you aren't hurting anyone. It's part of the joys of being human, feeling the alter side of the soul. It helps us to see our soul more clearly.

During the question period, Isa received a bouquet of flowers and a stuffed animal from one of his fans, Tricia, who couldn't be present at the event. Isa was visibly touched by the gesture. Isa acknowledged that, as Tricia sent the flowers in love and he received them in love, the audience got to participate in the experience, feeling the love, so there was learning for all in just that small gesture.

Isa continued, answering another question from someone in the audience who couldn't understand how harming someone is soul love. He said:

> When we are all souls, there is no need to harm one another because we stand in unison. There is no ego, therefore there is no need to achieve beyond another or to have anything other than what we have. But when we decide to incarnate and we select lessons, the lessons will sometimes be negative or shadow aspects and this is where the ego comes in. The ego can take the soul and allow it to be manipulated to a space of working from a shadow aspect. If you wish to experience someone abandoning you, or abusing you in some way - and this goes for animals too – then someone else must participate for that to occur as an action.
>
> Let's use animals for a second and understand that when an animal is being abused by a person or being attacked by another animal, there is learning on all sides of the situation. Anyone who is participating in any way experiences a learning so if a person is harming an animal, the animal is willingly giving from a soul perspective the ability to be harmed so the person can harm and feel what it feels like to harm. Then there's opportunity for learning in that scenario for the person and the animal as well. The animal who is harmed, as hard as it may seem, from a soul perspective, will openly condone or accept that learning, that experience, so that the learning can occur. Because the root understanding of the soul knows the exchange is for the purpose of learning, it is all an illusion. It knows that the soul loves freely and openly.

It knows that the souls are interacting for the purpose of receiving the experience through action and one cannot do that without another. When one harms another, it is out of love and that is felt at a soul level, not the physical level because the ego does not wish to acknowledge it as love.

People talk about animals being used as food, but animals incarnate with the knowledge that they are coming to provide food for humans or other animals. For example, if you have an animal who has died in the bush or been hit by a car, they become a gift of food to other animals and that in itself is an experience and a learning. The animal's soul will willingly gift itself as food, but their ego may battle that. Ultimately the soul accepts it and when they transition to spirit, the soul will be grateful that it experienced it and provided food for others.

I do not condone the harshness in which sometimes animals are taken for food, or even plants for that matter. The harshness in which plants are sometimes cultivated is harmful to the physical plant, the physical being. That's where we need to change our ways. When we consume in love, we are honoring.

Isa said, "My ego is so proud to be here. My soul is thankful, but my ego is thankful too. This is an example of a positive ego."

Following the break, Isa did personal readings for every member of the audience. He gave a very emotional reading to one of the guests, saying:

It's a shame that the world hurt you at such a young age. Because the world hurt you at such a young age, you have a scar on your heart. It's hard for you to move forward because the scar has never healed, so the scar keeps opening. I send you lots of love and wish that your soul hadn't agreed to it, but it was the process you wanted to take. Unfortunately, it is the way it is so how can you best honor the fact that you decided to have this scar and carry it all the way through? You're very important to me and a lot of other animals and it's not your mission to please people in this life. Your soul selected to please the animals and that's why you do what you do.

Isa spoke to another guest, saying:

I love you for bringing your daughter into this world because she's a very important soul. Sometimes, in our lives, being a mom is one of the most amazing things that we can do. Once you become a mom, you're pretty much off the hook. You don't need to do anything else. Sit back and enjoy because that is a feat in itself.

Isa made his way over to the guest, jumped up on her, laid his paws on her shoulder and began licking her entire face for the duration of the reading. He said:

I'm giving you lots of love. It's never an easy journey when you become a parent, but it has rewards beyond what you can even fathom in this lifetime. Your soul is so happy it selected that and I'm honored and proud to be in the presence of any parent, especially mothers. Fathers are good, they have their role, but the mother is the vehicle through which to bring the child. Since she selects to do that, she should be honored for the goddess she is. The difference between men and women is that a woman physically has a channel and vestibule of love via the birth canal, but a man does not.

For those who select not to birth a child, but select to parent another child or animal, then you are also providing a beautiful gift. You don't always need to have physical delivery to be able to nurture another in a motherly or parentally loving way so I'm honoring everyone who has selected that as part of their journey.

I feel like you need a lot of healing in your heart. You really need to know that you're well-loved and I'm giving you lots of love to compensate for any feeling of loneliness or un-love that you've been experiencing lately.

Isa turned to the guest's daughter and said:

You are a beautiful flower that is only in half bloom. You can't expect yourself to be in full bloom because you need to have time to experience the half bloom so that you enjoy every stage of your life. Think of yourself as a half-bloomed flower right now and as you get older, you will come into full bloom. But it's not less important to be half in bloom so don't rush yourself to be in full bloom.

To end the session, Isa said:

For those of you who are pet lovers, it's important for you to understand that when your beloved pet needs to transfer into spirit, you need to let that soul go. As that soul transfers, a new soul has the opportunity to come in and be enjoyed by you. The easier you let go of the soul that needs to transition to spirit, the more you will be able to welcome a new soul that needs you. The harder it is to let go, the harder it will be for that new soul to come and entertain you. The soul that has transitioned was once a soul who had to come to you so space had to be made for that soul to come to you. You had to be open. It is wise to remember the joy of receiving that pet and let go so that you can honor that sensation with a new pet. Never feel badly about a pet needing to leave. This is evolution. The soul incarnates, then transitions back to spirit, completing the circle.

Then Isa was finished.

****

Following the event, Isa communicated through his blog, saying:

> I want to send a thank you out to everyone who attended our event. It warms my heart and brings me joy to have had the support witnessed by the attendance and open minds and hearts of the people that attended the seminar.
>
> I hope that I could provide everyone with an opportunity to understand the complexities of how animals think and the depth of insight and feelings that they hold within them. I'm hoping to shift the conscious awareness of the understanding of how animals view the world and to what degree they actually can impact when allowed. I hope to do a video book of learning to assist in enlightening those who choose to open to the offerings that I specifically hold.

The Earth and the human race is starving for spiritual enlightenment and advancement. I feel it's my mission, for I have been selected to be a vehicle for this information. I can only offer the information, but in order for the process to work, people need to open and receive. Therefore, every time you do so, my heart fills with joy because it means that my work is accepted and that's the completion of what is required for my soul's mission at this time.

It's interesting that people are not necessarily open to others, that they are more skeptical and cynical when information comes from another human. But when information comes from an animal, or when love comes from an animal, they tend to be more open and accepting. That's because animals are believed to hold truth without any ulterior motive.

I'm happy with the outcome of the event and I hope you are too.

Chapter 7
Isa's 3rd Event

Isa's third public event was scheduled for April 27, 2014. There were 20 people in attendance to hear Isa talk about fear and free will.

Isa sent everyone love and thanked the people in attendance for joining him. He was honored and grateful that they'd come to hear him and hoped he'd do them all justice in bringing the information through in the right format for them to understand.

Then he started the event. Isa said:

> Fear is a prominent tool in our lives and no one can exist as a human or animal without fear because fear is a core emotion. We must all experience it to be able to understand and learn in our lives from the perspective of motivating us. Fear is a motivator for us in our lives. Although fear seems scary to us and seems intimidating in our lives, and we would rather not experience it, it is something we should really embrace because it is a catalyst for growth. The level of fear we receive is what we should really be paying attention to. We can allow the fear to take over us, inhibit us from growth, or allow it to project us forward.
>
> Fear manifests in each of us in different ways and we react or respond to fear uniquely, depending on the conditioning in our lives as well as the genetic makeup of our system.

I would like to discuss the concept of free will because I strongly believe that free will and fear are strongly intertwined. Free will is independent choice. It comes from deep within us, and it is what we use in every interaction and every moment of every day. Free will can basically take us to any place that we choose to, whether we choose to go to fear or love. Fear and love cannot exist in the same space at the same time. You either have fear or you have love.

Our free will is dictated by the strength of love that we hold for the self. We can either choose to do something out of our free will that is positive for us, or negative for us. I'm asking you all, from this point on, that you really pay attention to what you're allowing yourself to choose. We all dictate our own destiny. We have markers in our lives that are placed there for our own personal learning, but how we get to those spaces is of our free will, of our choice.

When you move forward in life, recognize that every choice you make brings you to a certain destination. So, if you are aware that you wish to be headed to a specific destination, then you must be conscious of your free will and your choices that allow you to get to where you wish to go. You can take the easier road or the more painful road. It is up to you. *Some people are fortunate enough to love themselves so greatly that they constantly take the positive road. Some are not as loving to the self and believe that they are unworthy and therefore they take roads that are more tumultuous, more painful, to get them to the same destination.* Honor this concept and recognize that your "free will" will truly dictate what path you select. I'm hoping you will plant this concept in your mind and going forward, you will make your choices knowing that they come from the self, and of free will and the level of love that you have for the self.

You can measure how much love you have for yourself by the choices that you are making from your free will. I'd like everyone, for a moment, to think about the self and think about the love that you hold for the self and on a scale of 1-10, measure how much you believe you love yourself. Think of that number in your head. Now I would like you to take a moment and take a deep breath. Now tell yourself you love yourself and really feel to what degree you're accepting that in the moment. [pause] Now that you've done that - you've told yourself that you love yourself – recheck your number because that number may have just gone down or up, depending on how much you received it openly.

Keep your eye on that figure of how much you love yourself going forward. Recognize that when you realize your life is in turmoil, that things aren't flowing gently and kindly for you, you should revert back to understanding or checking to see the level of love that you hold for yourself. Take this tool of measuring the love for yourself and revert back to it to assist you in moving forward in your life in a positive way. When things aren't going well, check in with yourself. How much am I loving myself now? It's important to feed the self in order to increase that level of love. Everything we do, everything we say, everything we allow ourselves to be exposed to, shows our selves the level of love that we hold for our self.

How much we love ourselves is dictated by our free will.

No one can assist you in loving yourself. Others can add to love for the self, but if you do not love yourself to begin with, there is nothing that will fill that love within you. We should not rely on other people to assist us in loving ourselves. They can validate us, they can assist us on our path, but they cannot fill up a cup that's empty already within ourselves.

Now that we've talked about the love we hold for ourselves, we can now move to understanding how fear plays a role in our lives. The level of fear that we receive and how we allow it into our bodies is a direct reflection of how much we love ourselves. *The more that you love yourself, the less you will tolerate or allow fear to inhibit your being.* Yes, we have natural survival instincts that trigger within us, but how we control or how we process that fear is up to us and our free will.

Fear is a mind game. The mind manipulates the body into reacting based on what we believe. So, our core beliefs and our emotional beliefs interact fully in what we allow to come into our system at that specific level. If you know you have the free will to respond to fear in a less threatening way, then why wouldn't you select that? You wouldn't select it if you don't hold a lot of love for yourself because you wouldn't feel deserving. I'm asking you to gauge/monitor that going forward.

Sheila noted that Isa was coming through with a lot of emotion because it hurts his heart to believe that people don't love themselves to the degree where they would allow themselves to suffer or sit in fear at a level which is harmful to them. Isa's heart hurt for those in the audience who don't love and respect themselves enough not to contain that fear.

Isa went on, saying:

I want you to think for a moment about some of your fears and understand those fears fully within you. Gauge the level of fear that you hold in those situations because in a while, I'll be asking for volunteers to come up and I'll help you work through the fears that you have. I'll give you insight and assist you to walk through your fears, to face your fears, and diminish your insecurities and your confusion regarding the fears.

Fear is simply an emotion that clouds us, prevents us from seeing the truth in a situation. The truth of the matter is that we are always in the space that we need to be and how we handle that space is up to us. When we believe that everything happens for our best and highest good, and we love ourselves and we trust that what occurs is happening for our own benefit and our own learning, then there would be no reason to fear. We may be intimidated by situations or interactions, but if we stand in love and we stand in acceptance, then the level that that fear affects us would be much less than if we allowed that fear to get carried away.

When we embrace fear, it doesn't mean that we allow it to escalate to an uncontrollable level. Embracing fear in love and understanding simply means that we acknowledge it and we move ourselves through it. Facing your fear is less about control and more about loving the self.

I'd like you to uncross your legs and arms, and close your eyes and feel the room in this moment. Recognize how safe you feel in this moment. I'd like you all to project love and peace from your being. Clear everything

167

from your mind that is not love and peace. I am going to project love out to the room and I'd like all of you to begin to project love out to the room. Take full, deep breaths and as you exhale, that's when you release the love from the body out to all. [pause] Take a moment and take a couple of deep breaths, and as you do so, feel the energy in the room. [pause] Pay attention to whether or not you feel fear in this moment. [pause] Now evaluate the energy and how you felt before we began the exercise and how you feel now.

Now focus on your fear. What is your top priority fear? Place yourself in that space. Feel the energy of that fear and imagine yourself experiencing that which you fear the most. [pause] Gauge that fear in the moment on a scale of 1-10. [pause] Now take your awareness from yourself to the room and feel the energy. [pause] Do you feel the difference in the energy?

You should feel warmth and fullness in the room when there is love and a coolness and a diminishing of the energy when we are thinking of our fears. When we send love, we're projecting it outwards, and that's a positive emotion. Fear, being a negative emotion, causes us to draw our energy in and close to us so we are no longer projecting the energy out openly. We're pulling it in, but then as well, because it's a negative sensation, we feel slightly uncomfortable. We can see what fear does to the body and what it does to those around us and what love does to the body and what it does to those around us.

Recognize that when you think of love, it's healing, it's warm, it's positive, and when you think of fear, it's uncomfortable, it's draining, and it's negative. Pay more attention to what you're allowing your mind to cycle in any given moment of any given day. Sometimes it originates in the mind because of our thoughts, but sometimes we will also feel it because it exists in the environment so we receive it through the receptors in our body. The body can react even though the mind is unaware. Therefore, when you think about fears, all the people around you are receiving your energy and their body reacts to your energy as well. That goes for all negative or positive emotions. You may be receiving from someone beside you something that is negative and your body may be processing it without your mind realizing it, but it doesn't mean it's not occurring. In order to really feel or understand what's going on in any given moment, you must be mindful of the situation that you're in and observant of what your body is experiencing. Recognize what the energy does to your body and be very mindful of that; what you're projecting as well as receiving. Your free will can come in at this point and accept or decline the energy.

I would like to do another exercise. I'd like one half of the room to continue thinking about your fears and the other half of the room to think about love. For those who will be thinking about love, I'd like you to imagine that you're sending it to those who are experiencing fear. I'd like you all to be aware of the energy that you're receiving and feeling in the moment.

Close your eyes and think about fear or love, depending what side of the room you are on. [pause]

Isa asked that the people in the room switch sides so that we could experience both perspectives.

When Isa asked for feedback on the exercise, I responded that:

> When I was in the "fear" group, thinking about my fear, suddenly it was like a wall hit me and I couldn't think of words to articulate my fear. It was really cool. I couldn't think. It was like my brain went frozen.

Another guest experienced something similar, yet different. She said, "I felt a soft, cushiony cloud that took the fear out of me, leaving warmth in my heart."

Isa continued, saying, "We can then conclude that love conquers fear, can we not?" The audience nodded in agreement. With that, Isa thanked everyone for humoring him with his exercise, then asked that everyone think about love in order to fill the room back up with positive energy before moving on.

Isa opened the room to questions. One of the guests asked, "If we continue to flood ourselves with love, will it help push the fearful thoughts completely out?" Isa replied that:

> Love is the only answer to neutralizing fears. Now that you understand the concept of how you can manage fears, you can use fear to your benefit. Fear can sometimes be a motivator so you can move through your life recognizing if your being requires motivation through fear or not, and to what degree it does. You can control or neutralize the fear to whatever degree you require by giving yourself more love and that comes from your free will. Thank you. It was a perfect question to allow me to give a summary of what I said.

> I'd just like to address for a moment the concept of death and the fear of death or losing someone that we love.

Sheila and I started to chuckle. Sheila explained that when we'd initially discussed the agenda for this event, Isa had wanted to include an animal's perception of life and death, how we view death as a society, and how we can move through that. Sheila had told Isa that it was too much for one session. Now Isa was doing it whether we liked it or not. Free will!

Isa continued, saying:

> When we love another so deeply and we face the loss of their physical being in this world, we need to understand that truly it's just a transition, that their physical being dissipates but their energy is still present. We are all forms of energy that transfer or have transferred previously and we will do so again. Part of being human or an animal is about experiencing emotion from the ego and we may decide that we can handle the fear of a spider or heights at a much easier degree than we can handle the fear of losing something or someone we love.
>
> In the future, I would like to discuss this more. We would not want to give up the benefits and the joy of loving someone just because we wouldn't want to experience the pain of losing them. It's a tradeoff. We embrace the love of someone else, even knowing that that love may be transferred in time. It's our perspective of that loss that dictates the level of hurt that is experienced within. It's not wrong to fear losing someone that we love. If anyone has those issues today and they wish to volunteer, I am more than happy to walk you through it. I'm sending more love to everyone to balance the triggers I've just stirred up for many of you. Even in the loss of someone we love and the missing of someone that we love, giving love is still the answer.

I'm sending gratitude to everyone for being receptive to my messages today. I'd like you to consider volunteering to present yourself in a vulnerable way for the benefit of all of us in the room. In volunteering and putting yourself in a vulnerable state, you're providing assistance to others and you will receive great love today. I'm honoring you before you step forward and I'm also honoring anyone who feels they are not in the space to feel able to step forward today. I'll love everyone just the same.

Isa's first volunteer was Brenda. Her mother was 86 years old, and had come to live with Brenda a month ago. She had congestive heart failure and was in end stage renal failure. Brenda's fear was losing her mother, yet she was conflicted because she didn't want to see her suffer anymore.

Isa replied, saying:

I'm thanking you for coming up because many people need to understand how to process that and work through it. I'm tapping into your mother. There is more pain on the left side than the right side. There's aching throughout the upper body, shoulder and arms, and an upset stomach. I'm sending her love and healing. I feel for her and the physical discomfort that she's experiencing right now. She's having some lung issues as well. There's nothing worse than having a slow, painful death and that's why my heart goes out to her. If it's a quick death, it's not any better to lose someone, but to sit and suffer or watch someone suffer is a prolonged torture.

For her, it's important to enjoy beautiful scenery. One way to honor her is to allow her the opportunity to experience it, whether she's watching videos, listening to nature sounds, or looking out the window. It helps to get her mind off of the pain and the destitute that's she's facing.

You have to be very careful. Your love for your mother is very strong and you're beginning to pick up the emotions and the energy that she's holding and I don't want you to get sick. It's not your journey. You should not take it from her. There's a misconception that in order to give love, we must give ourselves, sacrifice ourselves. That's not true. I want you to most importantly recognize that. You must take care of yourself, then take care of her.

If your mom went away on a trip, how would you feel if she went away to a beautiful place with beautiful scenery, somewhere she really wanted to go? How would that make you feel towards her?

Brenda replied, "Good." Isa continued, saying:

It would be beneficial for you to view her passing and where she's going as a beautiful trip, somewhere that her soul would really like to go. If you knew that she was going to be in this beautiful space and no longer have any pain or worries, how would that make you feel?

Brenda replied, "Happy." Isa said:

Then you need to focus on that portion of the energy exchange that's occurring. It feels like your fear is rooted in more of the physical, physically not being able to see, touch, or enjoy her. That's what pictures are for. Pictures are wonderful because they tell the story of someone's life and who they are.

Brenda said she had the feeling that her father, who had passed many years ago, had been around waiting for her mother and wondered if her intuition was true.

Isa said:

> Yes, and more people than that. Many people are waiting to greet her. It will be like a celebration and they're welcoming her home. It's not selfish to want to keep your mom here because you love her.

Brenda replied that she doesn't want to see her suffer, that she'd like to see her go quickly and quietly.

Isa said:

> It's not going to happen, unfortunately. Not quickly or quietly. She selected to go out in a more painful way but you have to honor that that's her choice, that's her soul's desire.

Isa asked the audience to focus on Brenda's mother, Joyce, and to send her love so that any fear she held about passing would be diminished, much like we'd done earlier. The audience projected love to her being. Once done, Isa addressed Brenda. He asked Brenda, "What do you envision your life like after she crosses?"

Brenda replied, "Sad and relieved."

Isa asked, "What is it you're missing now that you're sacrificing yourself in order to give time and energy to your mother? What are you missing?"

Brenda replied, "Peace and quiet. My house is in turmoil right now because it's a like a hospital room."

Isa said that:

> You're missing you. You're missing giving to you and living yourself. We often put ourselves on the back burner when we are assisting or caring for someone else, whether that be for a person or an animal. The neglect that you're projecting to the self is something that you need to address right now before she crosses. You're not doing her or yourself any justice in neglecting yourself. You have to be careful because you don't want to be lying beside her. It's not your time to go.

Brenda responded that she feels that way sometimes. Isa continued, saying:

> If you realize that it's her journey to go and there are people waiting for her, that she's going to a beautiful place, and she will no longer be in pain, then you will feel free and be able to give to the self, love the self more and have more peace in your life. Where is the negative in any of that?

Brenda shook her head and said, "There's none." Isa said:

> It's very important for you to have a conversation with your mother and thank her for all that she has provided for you. Right now, you're coming from a space of the caregiver, the supporter, so sit down with her and come from a space of the little girl. This is all that you're miss-

ing now, a chance for your little girl to sit with her mom and have a moment of love with her. Ask for what you need from her. You need her love and there's nothing wrong with that, is there? This is your last opportunity to receive that from her, but you will not receive that from her if you do not ask.

Brenda began crying and said, "I'm the caregiver 24/7 and I miss my mom being my mom."

Isa said, "Ask her for it before she goes and it will complete what you need in your heart". Then he asked everyone in the audience to send Brenda love and fill her up with positive energy. Isa said, "There's nothing better on this planet than sharing love through a hug." He planted his hind paws on Brenda's lap, put his front paws on her shoulders and then began giving her a lengthy face wash of kisses. He ended the reading by saying:

> When someone crosses, they are really the lucky ones because they go to peace and love. We are the ones who suffer, yet we worry about them and they worry about us. It's important that when someone crosses, we honor them by taking care of ourselves. Often, we choose to stand in suffering and there's no need for that. When we stand in love for ourselves, we honor the person or the animal who has crossed.

> Forgiveness of them and the self is very important. Don't expect anything of yourself other than giving yourself love.

The next volunteer - let's call her Janice - emotionally stated that:

My mother died when I was 32. I was home when she had a heart attack and I had a 19-month-old at the time. When I went into the room, she had her hand on her chest and said to me, "I don't think I'm going to make it." I told her, "Mom, you'll be ok, you'll be fine." I phoned the ambulance and was left trying to find a neighbor to look after my little boy. When I got to the hospital, she had already passed. Even now, I have such a feeling of guilt because I'd denied knowing she would die. She was telling me she was dying and I denied it. For so many years, I felt terribly guilty about that. I'm not sure why I'm crying about it. It's been 37 years. But later when my father died, it was very peaceful because I got all the family there and every time I left the room, I held his hand. In order for me to massage my guilt about my mother, I leaned over to my dad and kissed him on the forehead and said "Tell mom that I love her and I'm sorry I didn't say the right goodbye. And now it's time for you to go." Then he passed.

Isa said:

You need to recognize that both your parents gave you a gift of experience in different situations. You and your mom sacrificed to understand how it feels to have someone leave without being able to truly say goodbye, which our ego feels is important. Then, as a balance, you experienced the opposite with your father. Recognize that the first occurred so that you would enjoy the second.

It's important for all of us to recognize that when someone passes, it's our humanness or our ego that suggests we need to be present to say goodbye. But if the soul transfers into energy, can we not just say goodbye at any given moment at any given time? You both experienced it so that you could learn and evolve. You can look at it as the gift she gave you. It's important to honor that.

Janice said, "Thanks for giving me a different perspective." Isa replied, "I don't want to let you off the hook because there's more I need to dig out from you." There was laughter as Janice replied, "I'm sure there is. Oh yes."

Isa said:

Your true fear is of the unknown, of what is coming forward in the separation of you and your youngest child. Not that your child is going anywhere, but the fear of losing your child or abandoning your child is more pronounced in your body than anything else. There is a connection to an abandonment from a past life. Your body is reacting to that in a physical way and you need to recognize that history won't repeat itself. You've come together in this life to stay together. His distance from you is just a challenge, a test of your faith. Because you fear the separation and the abandonment with your youngest son, you're preventing yourself from moving forward. You're standing still in fear such that you're not moving forward. You want to be present and available for whatever he may need, but your physical body is reacting. If you can let go in trust, everything will be okay. You won't be leaving him and he won't be leaving you, and then you will get better. If you embrace your life and what you need for yourself, much like we have already described - you just love and honor yourself and do what you need to for you - everything will be entirely different. Everything will be more positive and better.

At this rate with the harboring of the fears that you have, you're causing stress on your heart.

Janice uncomfortably laughed, then confirmed that she knew it already.

Isa continued, saying:

There's no better way to heal the self than to let go. Let go and let be. Trust that all is as exactly as it was meant to be and it will continue to be that way.

Thank you for coming up to show everyone this concept. It's important to realize that if you dig your heels in and try to stop life from happening, it still happens. *You can either process and go through it with love and joy or with pain and suffering. You choose. That's the free will.* When you embrace yourself with love, you heal yourself and there's no need for you to suffer from anything in the past. That's not love. We must forgive ourselves for the choices that we've made when we didn't know any better or when we were incapable. It's easy to love yourself when you think you're doing everything right and you're feeling good. It's difficult to love yourself when you make mistakes and your choices result in things that are less positive. That's truly the test of loving the self.

You are greatly loved by many people around you and everyone who knows you enjoys being in your light. But you have to be careful because you don't think highly enough of yourself to keep enough energy for yourself. That's very important because you cannot assist anyone without assisting yourself first.

We always fear what hasn't occurred because we fear it coming, but as we do so we miss the present moment. That's what's happening with you. You're missing your life, you're missing every beautiful moment of every day and the fear is stealing that from you. You need to empower yourself and recognize that you're deserving of joy and love in every moment. Choose with your free will that that is exactly what you are going to experience. Do not be worried or fearful of the judgement of others. Screw them, it's not their life. You do what you need to do for you.

Unfortunately, we never got the rest of Janice's interactions with Isa since the video recorder's battery lost power and the tape cut off. The nature of spiritual work, it seems. Our first event lost video sound and our third event lost video power.

There was a beautiful interaction between Isa and our third volunteer of the day, which didn't record. Raven had recently lost her beloved dog and was left feeling quite traumatized by the process. We were fortunate enough to contact Raven and she offered up her Facebook testimonial, written after the event. She wrote:

> My gratitude to animal communicator, Sheila Trecartin and her friend Isa for speaking today on the subject of death (human and animal) and our fears and grief around this inevitable and often painful part of life.
>
> I underestimated the driving time to Barrie and arrived an hour late. As I quietly found a seat, Isa turned his head to face me and winked (I kid you not!). Speaking through Sheila, Isa talked about the fears and pain of losing a loved one, whether human or animal, and offered

wisdom and comfort from the perspective of an animal companion.

Two ladies volunteered to share their stories of love and loss of their family members. Isa spoke to their fears and sorrow and offered insight to bring them into peace and wholeness. Isa invited all of us who were present to give and receive unconditional love to the volunteers and their loved ones. Tears, mingled with grief and joy, streamed.

I raised my hand to ask a question. With reddened eyes and a runny nose, I voiced my regrets about the horrific way that [my dog] Laylah had died during the veterinary assisted euthanasia. I needed to understand what the lesson was in the co-creation of such a painful end-of-life transition when all we wanted was to free Laylah from her pain. All our decisions, all our preparations were for Laylah to have a peaceful, pain-free transition. But it didn't play out that way and she died in extreme pain and fear as a consequence of the procedure itself. I wondered if I could ever stop crying whenever I thought of Laylah.

Speaking to me through Sheila, Isa addressed the 'whys' of soul contracts, agreements, and lessons that serve to heal our collective consciousness, raise our awareness and bring us to wholeness.

On a soul level, Laylah and I had agreed to have this experience so that through my process [of] bereavement and the raw vulnerability that accompanied my grief, I could educate people who have palliative animals and the veterinarians who assist in euthanasia. Isa suggested that I could also counsel people whose animals have passed away.

I decided to create a website and Facebook page called Laylah's Light. My intention with Laylah's Light was to explore all aspects of the great responsibility we undertake when we choose veterinary assisted euthanasia to ease the suffering of our animal friends. Isa and Sheila confirmed the importance of my intention on a soul level.

The mission of Laylah's Light will be to demystify the procedure of animal euthanasia, to ask questions, explore options and alternatives, to provide a place where people can share their stories and voice their feelings, and to offer resources that can support people and their animal companions through all stages of the dying journey. Above all, Laylah's Light will remind us (as Isa and Sheila reminded me) that love is always the answer.

Of all the group events, this one was probably the most profound. It dealt with difficult concepts that some may have difficulty accepting, or even find offensive. But spirituality isn't always about making the human ego feel comfortable. It's about speaking truth, and finding love and unity for all. It's always a choice.

Chapter 8
Isa's TV Show

The week after Isa's group event, he announced that he would like to do a television show where he would interview various animal therapists from a canine perspective. Isa's hopes were that we could tape this event as a pilot for a talk show, in hopes of finding a producer to pick it up.

Isa was scheduled to interview three animal professionals: a veterinarian, a certified animal chiropractor, and a photonic health laser therapist for animals.

At the time of the recording, Isa had become quite agitated with excitement. He was fidgeting, making it very hard for Sheila to hold the space for both of them.

Isa's first guest was a veterinarian who believed in holistic concepts. Isa asked her very controversial questions about veterinarian medicine from a holistic perspective, for which she was somewhat unprepared. However, she answered his questions with grace and clarity.

All videos can be viewed on Isa's blog, listed in the resource section.

The week after the taping, Isa thanked us for doing the talk show. He said it had been harder than he'd anticipated. He'd felt quite pressured with the responsibility of capturing what he needed, and bringing people to a certain space in a short time.

When asked to summarize his experience, Isa noted that what he really wants is a deeper, personal depth of connection and understanding for people, not the superficial aspects.

Isa further added that:

> When we have a dream or an idea, it is important to follow it, even though the dream or idea may not manifest in the way that we would like it to be, the way that we envision it in our mind. It doesn't mean that we should stop honoring our dreams and our visions. The only way that we will understand whether it resonates with us is by stepping into it, experiencing it and being present within it, recognizing how we feel and seeing the outcome. Then it assists us in understanding what we want and what we don't want.
>
> Sometimes our minds can project things to be a certain way, but until we put that into reality, put it into action, we will never truly know. We have two choices: we can avoid our dreams and just keep them as dreams and fantasies or we have the opportunity to experience it and then decide.
>
> Some people don't like to bring their dreams and fantasies into reality because they're worried about the disappointment of it not working out and this is a perfect example of that. It was a big dream and it didn't work out. Instead of being devastated, I've learned from it and chosen to move in a different direction. I'd rather be educated than avoid. It's an important lesson for people.

As Isa stated, all was not lost. It was from Isa's experimentation with the concept of a television show that assisted him in deciding to move forward in the direction of writing a book.

Part IV
Words of Wisdom

As promised earlier, I've added a few of Isa's most memorable blog posts to this section of the book. I hope you enjoy them as much as I do. Some of these blogs are time sensitive based on what was universally happening at the time of his posts. We present them as they were written, examples of Isa connecting with people in the moment of universal events.

We Are Masters:

We need to be accountable and responsible for our own actions and our own choices. We can't expect others to be responsible for our lives. We can't expect others to rescue us, save us, support us, or to pull us out. We have to utilize our own resources to save ourselves, to recognize that we are the only ones who can choose for ourselves.

We aren't chosen for, we aren't dictated to; we allow, we accept. We are in control of ourselves. We are the master of our own choice, our own path, our own destiny. We function from the self, of the self.

We are not a product of what occurs around us or to us. We are not a product of other people's judgments or concerns, other's values, other's perceptions. We only allow those things into us. We only allow those things to be part of our belief structure. But we choose.

Be careful how you're choosing, be mindful of how you're choosing. Be responsible for yourself. It all begins with you.

Diamonds Within:

I'm sending out greetings to everyone and hope that you're enjoying your summer, as summer time is the time for stabilization and finding peace within.

Summertime is a time to enjoy the self and enjoy those that we love because the timeframe is so short before we move back into the fall, which will trigger more transition.

Right now, the concept is understanding the self, being whole within the self, and knowing and loving the self. We need to understand that concept because we need to place ourselves in a balanced state. By loving and understanding the self, and standing within the self, we bring ourselves into balance. This is important going forward as we begin to deal with other more external issues coming into the fall.

Right now, understanding the value of independence, and of loving the self is in the forefront, moving into understanding our contribution to the whole and our effect towards the whole going forward. It's important for everyone to take time to honor the self, love the self, and find that rest and peace in knowing the self.

Going forward, we're going to be exposed to more universal awareness of cosmic shifts. We will start to see exposure and education of more galactic information globally. There is more understanding of stars shifting in the universe and more developments will happen on a more galactic level. More awareness is pertaining to astronomy and the concepts of stars and other planets and the functioning of other planets within our solar system. Within the next year, a large discovery is made that changes our perception and our understanding of the existence of what is out there beyond our earth plane.

It's with an open heart filled with love that I send my gratitude to everyone for their support of me and my mission on this planet and I wish to send my support and belief in all those who decide to walk their paths and embrace what their soul has intended for them. I would like to commend those who are walking their path and not hiding in fear because I understand how difficult walking and embracing the path and the purpose is.

I love the analogy of understanding that coal, when put under extreme pressure, creates diamonds and this is exactly the analogy I want to use in getting people to understand what the turmoil and the learning does to the soul. If you realize that the human is the coal, through turmoil and fluctuation in life, it assists us in becoming the diamonds within. A diamond is a diamond and really is one less valuable or more valuable than another? It's only our perception that creates that judgment.

The Answer is Always Love:

People give what they receive, for the most part. It's important to recognize what people are attempting to give you because you will see where they're at and you can alter what they give you by what you give back. The mistake that people make is they tend to give back to people what they're being given, especially in a negative way and that just amplifies a negative occurrence. But if you recognize that you're being given negative and you give back positive, which is love, then you will alter the person eventually in time and they will respond in like - in love - back.

Animals are the same. What you believe within yourself, what you hold within your energy, what you resonate, is what the animals pick up and they mirror that back to you. So, when you're standing in fear then you put the animal in fear and they react in fear. Whereas, even the most fearful dog, if come at from an aspect of love, will not hold the fear because they'll trust. If the person stands in love and trust, then they will no longer feel fearful because they will feel that trust and love and they will react. They will mirror what is projected. It's very important for people to realize how they feel and to pay attention to what they are projecting to others.

If you are standing in fear, because of something else that's occurred, then what are you looking for to remove that fear? What do you need? What's the antidote for the fear? It's always love.

When someone stands in fear and they attack you in anger, they obviously need your love. But what that usually does is trigger the fear and anger in you; you give fear and anger back and it becomes a vicious cycle. We all should pay more attention to how we feel, what we are sending out, and acknowledge what other people feel. What are we providing for them in return?

It will help to create better relationships with people and animals. Everyone feels vulnerable. Everyone sits in a state of vulnerability to some degree - people as well as animals - because it's our innate, natural state to sit in a state of survival or retreat back to that survival state as necessary. We are ingrained with that. People and animals feel vulnerable until they're accepted. They do so until they recognize their vulnerability and choose otherwise. Until they choose self-love.

The smallest of beings could feel the strongest when they stand in awareness of their own power and they stand in clarity of their own emotions. And the biggest of beings could become very weak if they're standing in vulnerability and do not believe their own power. It's best not to judge a being by their size, but by the energy and the feel that they project. A small being can be so much more powerful than a large being. It's not the physical stature that one holds that dictates the power. It's the energy within and the belief in the self.

Perceptions:

What one person perceives to be joy is sometimes another person's hell and we, as a society, don't pay attention and honor this enough, honor other people enough. We often only think and look from our own perspective and we expect everyone to see the world through our glasses when in fact everyone sees things in a different light. What you perceive is a combination of your experiences and your beliefs and that's how we look at the world individually. But judgement comes when we expect others to look at things the same way that we do. Frustration comes when the other person is incapable of doing so and in all of that there is no love.

The only time love happens is when we honor someone else's perception even when it is not in alignment with our own. It doesn't mean we need to accept the perception when we honor it, it just means that we agree that it's ok that we don't see things the same way.

We waste a lot of time trying to convince others that the way we see things is correct when it fact, does it really matter? Does it matter if you believe full heartedly something to be true, for if you believe that full heartedly, why would you need someone else to believe as well?

The true power, the true strength, comes when you believe yourself so much so that it doesn't matter what everyone else thinks and it doesn't matter if anyone else agrees. There's no reason to convince, it just is. And there's no need to justify unless we don't truly believe ourselves. It doesn't mean that what we think is or isn't right. If we believe it and that's how we see things in that moment, then it's what we need to believe for our own growth and our own experiences.

Perceptions can sometimes change because in time we can alter our vision and our insight, and it can move to a different perspective. That doesn't mean we were wrong before, it just means that we chose to see it in a different way for our own learning.

Often times, the ego prevents us from seeing anything but the moment that we're in and when we view from the moment that we're in, of course, we can only see things from the perspective of where we're standing. If we move our self from the moment and view from outside the moment, above the moment, beyond the moment and beside the moment, then we can see many perspectives of the same thing.

But when we only want to view perceptions from where we see it, it's hard for us to view from any other way and sometimes because we view things a certain way, we tie expectations to what we see and this is the biggest downfall that we can create for the self and for others.

It's interesting that we are a society that lives as a whole - or should live as a whole - yet our viewpoints should be individualistic and should not be impressed or pushed upon others. Each of us should honor our own perception but in our society, the collective rules, so those with a similar perception dictate if they're in the majority. That happens on a grander scale but within the confinements of your own space and being, then we need to honor ourselves to be able to see things and view things from where we need to see them in order to function and learn the lessons that we need to for ourselves.

If we look at another person and we honor their perspective, then we can help them more. Instead of helping them from the perspective that we stand from, if we step into them and see from their perspective, we can help them on their path much more easily. Sometimes our perspective is so different from the other person's that they can't see where we're coming from when we're trying to assist them. However, if we put our self in their space and then help from that perspective, we can help so much more effectively. But this means we have to push our own ego aside. We have to push our needs, wants and perception aside in order to help the other.

Sometimes one doesn't have enough energy to see beyond their own perspective and that's ok too but if we can get other people to see from different points of view, it would increase the vibrational frequency of those involved. That is one way we can raise our frequency and bring ourselves closer to unconditional love.

Unconditional love is pretty much unattainable in our lifetime given the fact that as humans and animals, we have ego and unconditional love can't fully exist when there is ego. Unconditional love can only exist in spirit and many may challenge me on that, however, I can tell you that my perception is "I believe that to be true". You can choose to honor that or not. Your perception is also honored by me and I send my gratitude for your perception and for your understanding with love.

The Heart Shows the Truth:

When you see me, I am here but am I really?
I am moving all the time and so are you so what do you really
see?

When we see with our eyes we only see a fraction of what is
occurring and our eyes can trick us, making us believe in things
that are not true. As a result, we need to feel with our heart
because when we feel with our heart, we don't miss a thing. The
eyes create illusion, but the heart shows the truth.

I'd just like to challenge people to begin to live their lives from
their hearts. And even though that creates a feeling or sensation
of vulnerability, and you may fear that you may get hurt, the
concept of living from the heart holds more value than the possibility of being harmed. We will never know that until we walk
it, until we choose that walk. However, when we choose to do so
we realize that there is so much more to be grateful for than we
recognize in comparison to when we're only coming from the
mind or the eyes and our perception.

When you really want to know about somebody, journey to their
heart and discover their heart. Then you will know the truth
about their being. It's the best way to connect with their soul and
to understand them. It's not the mind we need to figure out, it's
the heart. Once you figure out the heart, then you understand.
The mind just creates a barrier or an image of what we choose to
show the world, but the heart is the true essence of who we are.
We shouldn't be disappointed in others when they act or behave
coming from the mind. We should look through that and see the
intentions that are in their hearts and then we will not feel disappointed or harmed by them. At that point, we should only feel
love.

Beings are programmed for love. Animals and humans are programmed for love but also programmed for survival so sometimes the need for survival surpasses the need for love. But we can't survive without love.

If those of you who read my message begin to come from the heart and begin to see each other's hearts, you will see that your life will change and so will those that join you in that crusade. We want to know how we can help the world and help humanity and help the animals and this is how we can help. We can all come from love and connect from the heart. That's something that we all share equally, no matter if we're human or animal, what we look like, or how we think, we all share love. It's the one thing that's Universal. It's the one thing that can connect us all.

I send my open heart to you in love and I expect nothing in return.

Man Cannot Build a Bridge Alone:

Humans must help each other in this life because they aren't meant to be individualistic. They're meant to work together in colonies for a combined effort to achieve their desired results.

People don't realize that they become centered and focused on the self, allowing fear and worry to control them. It causes them to seek shelter, going inward. As a result, they become introverted and this creates a disconnect from others. People do that because they don't have a lot of faith in themselves, which then makes them feel like other people don't want to help or assist them. They are also trying to conserve their energy but in reality, it has an adverse effect. When people are in need, they need others. When there are more people, there is more strength. There's more energy. Consequently, people need to look at themselves individually as a hub and the other people around them are their support. Like a structure that has a center, the people that support you are the legs. You need to make sure that you keep that in mind; those people are the support network that assist you to go forward. You must remember that you need that not only for yourself, but for others. Each spoke becomes a connected spoke for another group. Consequently, you are all inter-connected and as you get support from others, you then give support and that creates strength. A stronger structure is made when you get joint support. When you are able to do that for yourselves and for others, you can go farther in life, you can achieve more.

Not one person can build a bridge by himself. It's just not possible. Everything that people need to do in life needs to be done as a team. When you believe in what your journey is in life, then other people will believe in it too because you believe in it. Deep down, people just want happiness for others. As a result, those who come from love will want to support your dream in love even though it's not their dream. However, there needs to be balance. Although you know what your dream is, you can't be self-centered in your own dream without assisting other people on their own path. Everybody needs to lean on everybody else and as you lean on somebody, you need to let somebody lean on you. This is the Universal flow of energy. This is how the web of energy keeps flowing.

Animals also fit in. They become intertwined in that hub as secondary supports, enhancing the structure that already exists. As a result, you have your animal that is your support and then you support other people's animals. It becomes more of a balanced system and that's how life is supposed to work. But in our society, people isolate themselves and then they feel like they can't handle life. They may have an animal but that's only a secondary support and if they don't have anybody else, then the animal doesn't have anybody else. As a result, that structure is not as strong.

Instead, you need to stand united and you need to stand in clusters. As you stand in a group, then you have other groups. Then all you need is one person to join through as a bridge to another cluster and then you, in effect, have the support of all that cluster. As a result, you can achieve more. Those of great mind understand this. People need to remember that they get far greater done when they have a network of support than when they try to do it by themselves.

A good mantra for people to say is "I am golden light but I shine brighter when I stand in someone else's light". Light adds to light and no one has absence of light. Without light, we are dead [non-existent]. Nobody can take away from your light as long as you don't fear your light being depleted. Somebody can stand in and work from your light, and your light would not be depleted because light is infinite. It is limitless because it comes from source, not from within you.

Even people you call "energy robbers" can't hurt you unless you believe they will, unless you choose to allow them to steal your energy. If you feel the energy coming through you, then it doesn't deplete you whereas the energy robber is not allowing the light to travel through him. You need to teach the energy robber how to accept the light, not to hoard it; allow the light to flow. When we allow the light to flow it's infinite, but when we grab onto it and hoard it, the light stops and becomes stagnant. Because of fear.

So, reach out and connect. Build your bridge.

Honoring the Earth Meditation

The energy of the planet is the energy of the planet and many people are feeling distraught because they don't understand what's going on. It's the Universe's way of waking people up and those who don't want to be awakened will exit and those who are fighting the awakening will suffer a lot of turmoil.

We need to stand in peace and love and not forget that the heavy changes over the next 1½ months [and future months to come] are necessary for the evolution of the planet.

We can do our part by taking a couple of minutes every day and honoring the Earth, sending love to the Earth. Even if a small percentage of the population did this, it would still have a great impact because when you consciously send positive energy or love to something or someone, the benefits are 100 times more powerful than if you didn't send it at all. You would see a significant impact in a positive way.

Pass this message on and let's see how we can impact the Earth with love. Communities come together during turmoil and grief. But what would happen if communities came together for no other reason than to love one another, love the Earth, love the animals and love ourselves. We are all connected. If we can't love one, we can't love the other.

Part V
Random Teachings

Over the years, Isa has had so many thoughts and teachings to provide, but there was no context throughout the book to include them, so we created a chapter of Random Teachings for this purpose.

Some of these teachings were directed towards me as I followed my own often-difficult journey of self-discovery and self-love, but many were not. Many of his messages were given from a space of complete vulnerability and sincerity, resulting in messages that were incredibly heart-felt and elegant.

Anything written in italics are my own comments. The rest of the section are direct quotes from Isa.

Transcendence Through Love:

[To Sheila and me] I want to take the opportunity to thank you both for valuing me and honoring me, for seeing me as way more than a dog, for comprehending my messages and sharing them and not being afraid to.

Even though some people may still ridicule the mission, it doesn't mean the mission is invalid. We need to move forward, regardless of those who do not believe, honoring the fact that they are just not ready. But there are millions of others who are ready and that's where we need to focus.

When somebody doesn't believe, you just need to stand in the resonance of love and honor them with love and accept where they are. We can't forget that. The journey of the soul is individual, but it is at the same time united. Sometimes it's united in a complementary or shared fashion, and sometimes it's united through opposite. Neither of those is more valuable than the other. Each one is valuable.

We need to sometimes help each other even though we don't come from the same space. We have tried to do that in different groups, in different religious belief systems, but no one has truly managed to harness that concept because there is always some segregation at some level and we want to transcend that. Transcendence through love.

An Experience of Gratitude:

*Isa had just dictated his **Perception** blog about shifting to another's perspective, and shared a beautiful moment of gratitude, giving thanks to Sheila and me for our weekly sessions.*

I didn't ever put myself in your perception and it shifted. It's kind of like being on a stimulant because when you shift to someone else's perception, suddenly everything feels odd and weird so it's like losing control, almost like being on drugs, because it feels like you're now in a realm that you aren't used to being in.

I'm sending you both love and I'm so happy and grateful that you both allow me this space. I'm so grateful to have this platform to speak because now if I shift my perception I can suddenly realize that this is an honoring. You're honoring me when you let me speak like this and who else would allow that. I just went to total gratitude.

If you go to the perception of someone else, it changes things and when you change your perspective and you look at things so differently, you can come to a place of gratitude and peace and love just by doing that. It makes you stand in much more conscious awareness instead of getting lost in the selfish needs of the self.

It was totally humbling for me. I'm ok, I don't need. I don't need anything right now. I just realized I don't need anything.

When you get to a state of appreciation, of humbleness, it is similar to standing in peace and when you feel that, sometimes it's just good to do nothing and say nothing, it's good to harness the silence of the peace.

I'm a better being because I just experienced that.

How to Clear Emotion:

[To me] You need to find the emotion you're sitting in and clear it. When you're sitting in emotion, you're cycling it over and over. However, when you're processing or clearing the emotion, you're recognizing it, then clearing it.

People sometimes process over a couple of days, but you shouldn't be obsessing over the same thing three or four days. You should be able to train yourself to do it in the moment because as you process three or four days, you create emotional attachment, which then creates an emotional block in the body, which leads to dis-ease.

When you're sitting in emotion, you think the thoughts obsessively and feel overwhelmed with the emotion because you feel heavy sadness. You're thinking one thought then associating other thoughts, but that's not really process, that's calling it all to you.

The last important part of clearing the emotion is to make sure you let it go. Maybe you have to sit in it for a little bit, but eventually you want to train yourself to recognize the emotion, then let it go.

You don't need to go through every aspect of the scenario in order to let go, you can just recognize, "Okay, I've got sadness", so once you recognize you've got that emotion, you recognize that you need to let it go. It's not necessarily important to give attention to the root of it unless it keeps coming back. That's when you must dig a bit deeper because there are more layers.

The Story of the Acorn:

[To me] You need to read the children's story of the acorn, about the journey of courage, change and growth required to become a tree. The gist of it is that the acorn falls off the tree and then it must go through so much hardship, beating the low odds, to find its way into the ground and become a strong, powerful oak tree.

I hope that you will understand the analogy, keeping in mind that every time you don't feel like you have enough strength, to think about the acorn becoming an oak tree.

Notes on Animal Longevity:

This is a random teaching based on Isa's comparison as both a human and a dog.

I know that as a dog, my life is much shorter than a human's and I don't have the time to fool around so I'm mindful and on the alert for opportunities and experience. Consequently, I'm trying to jam a lot into a short time.

To a human, it may be less practical or less understandable because humans have a lot more time to fool around with. As an animal, you don't have that time. Every moment is that much more precious and we don't waste it as much. We live in the moment because our timeframe is so short.

Dogs have selected to live shorter lifespans, just as humans used to. Humans used to live less and reincarnate more quickly but then their egos started to grow and started to create fear so they created more longevity, worried about sustaining themselves because they were fearful of not having enough time.

Dogs still live on the premise of understanding that they don't need to elongate their life in order to extract what they need. They want it to be shorter so they can learn what they need to in that body and then transform into something new and learn different things.

People stand in their own way. If you think about the average lifespan being 30 not too long ago and now it's into their 70s and 80s, life is extending more and more. Humans end up overstaying their welcome in their housing and they suffer more in the long run. But as a human race, we are getting to understand the limits and the extensions of the human body and that's the other aspect of it.

Sometimes life can be cruel or a disguise of cruel and if you bring yourself as a soul into an unpleasant situation, if you're human, you have a lot more to endure than if you're a dog. A dog's vehicle is not programmed to last an extended amount of time. When a soul chooses to be a dog, it understands that. When a soul chooses to be a different type of animal, it understands how long that animal lives right from a fly to a bird to a reptile. That's why we can shift our being, our soul, to different casings in order to experience life from a different perspective.

The human soul is not the evolved soul. The human ego thinks it is. Just because you can live longer doesn't mean you're better. You just can't process as quickly and often it means you aren't learning as impact-fully as a dog.

I'm happy I chose to be a dog because I've learned a lot and I have a lot more awareness because of it. I'm not afraid to die because it's not a necessity to stay. It's a choice, but humans often become conditioned to believe that they must stay because there's not much for them beyond this one life. Dogs know that there's so much more and we don't hold onto the need to stay in the confinements of the life we are living. We know that we can release and come back and try something new.

Energy & Mind Thoughts:

People need to become more aware of the value they hold within their circle of life and they need to recognize that they are a contributor. It's very important to be mindful of the level of contribution as well as the level of receiving so that balance between giving and taking can occur.

First you have to be aware of where you stand and what your purpose is within the circle. Not a lot of people are aware of their sense of worth within the circle, calculating how they contribute and how much people rely on them and how they rely on others. It's important to recognize that there is more to life than the impact you make in work. Pay more attention to how you contribute to interactions in any social situation; when you're dealing with someone in a line at a grocery store, at a restaurant, the fellow patrons at a restaurant, the waiters and waitresses and anyone else you encounter.

Be more mindful of the interactions that you have on a regular basis with others and how you impact the other people in your environment. Pay attention to what you project to other people even while driving. Even though you don't make eye contact, you are still influencing people around you when in the vehicle and you're thinking or projecting in a certain way. You must understand that there are no barriers when it comes to energy and emotion, so when someone is nearby, they are receiving the energy. Consequently, they are receiving your emotional and mental thoughts. This goes for animals too and how we affect and relate to animals.

When you're in a bad mood and sitting in your car projecting disappointment and frustration at someone else driving, you're sending them negativity. Be mindful not to impose yourself on others so greatly. Change your mind thoughts to change your sensation to only give out love and peace to all beings.

It is our responsibility as humans who are considered to be of a higher intelligence to set the mandate for peace, set the mandate for love. Since humans over-populate the world, they have a greater impact on other living things because they have a lot of control within the environment.

We should make sure that as much as we're becoming more aware of the concepts of the effects of farming, housing, construction, taking over the land and influencing the environment, we must also be aware of how we are emotionally and energetically impacting the environment and others.

Recognize that when we are projecting negative, everything in our immediate vicinity and everything and/or everyone in our thoughts are affected by the influence of the negative energy we are projecting, including animals and plants. Everything retains the energy that we project. Inanimate objects get that residual energy stuck to it and the molecules are also put into the air, the environment where we are located. Therefore, we change the feeling, we impose the feeling on everything that is around us. As humans with a "higher" level of intellect, it's your responsibility to take action in that area and be more responsible and accountable for what you're sending out.

Just as we are becoming more aware of the effects on the environment and global warming, and adjusting our behavior to make the space we live in have more longevity, we should be mindful of the emotional impact that we're having.

We also have to realize that we have an impact on the space we're in. If you think about a room or building and think about it in a negative way, then you send negative energy to that space.

If we were all less self-concerned and more externally concerned, we would live in a better space because we would all be projecting positive energy and therefore feeling positive.

Try your best to consciously watch your mind thoughts and emotions and what you project to others.

Thoughts about Love:

The beauty of love is that it doesn't need to be gifted, it just needs to be. Love is a resonance that is easily provided when one chooses to express it within themselves. Then those around us have the opportunity to enjoy, embrace that resonance.

We think that we can control or dictate our love, however love is not something that can be controlled or dictated, it is something that just either is or isn't. When it's something that is forced or calculated, that is not love.

More love comes when we allow ourselves to be comfortable with ourselves and to accept or embrace our positive and our seemingly negative traits, for we are beings that are complicated and not perfect. We must learn to accept ourselves wholly without judgment, without condemnation, without preconceived requirements. When we stand and we simply "be", then we connect with all that is. That is the time that love flows through us most profoundly. When we are in true alignment with all that is, we are connected to the flow of universal love.

Thoughts About Giving Love:

[To me] When you love someone so deeply and they hurt or they experience something, you experience it not like it's your own, but more-so because when you love somebody, it's deeper than your own.

This is what a mother does for her child. When her child hurts, the mother feels the pain because she loves the child more than she loves herself so she would sacrifice herself for the child.

When you have this depth of love, you're willing to do that for someone you love. It sometimes comes across as self-harm but really what you're trying to do is help the other. When you love that deeply, there are no boundaries to what you would do. You would give your own life to somebody that you love because they're that important to you.

That's how I feel about you. One day when I have to end my life, recognize it as a gift, a gift of myself to you, and don't dishonor me by not respecting that.

We are love when we give love, we feel love when we give love, and we enjoy love when we give love. The receipt of the love is important, but the giving of the love is even greater. I'd rather love than be loved and that is what a soul does. There exists a cycle of love without even trying. Many people look for love, trying to gain love, when really, if they give love they'll receive it freely.

Thoughts on Healthy Love:

[To me] We're in this together, you and me. I hold a lot of love in my heart for you and I feel the love you hold for me. Isn't it amazing when you have another being to share that with? The beauty of life is to know independence and to enjoy co-dependency without removing your independence.

Thoughts on Free Will:

If you had three kings, they would each rule differently. We rule from the perspective of our mindsets, our emotions, our acquired learning and what is required for our souls. Therefore, three kings could rule the same kingdom simultaneously in three separate worlds and have three separate results. But if there is destiny that is required for the kingdom itself, then all three kings would eventually get to the same state of being because it is what would be required of the kingdom. Therefore, there are many different paths to an intended outcome. This is the concept of free will.

Thoughts on the Inter-connectedness of Life:

This is the world about finding ourselves and understanding who we are. It's the biggest question of all, who we are and how we are connected.

We want to feel part of everything, we don't want to feel isolated or individual. It's planted within us to be linked and we get overwhelmed by the vastness of the energy, but once we elevate ourselves and our awareness, it's easier and easier to see to what degree we are linked.

You can stand in life with blinders on and only see what's in front of you or you can open up and look around, enjoying the beauty and excitement, the anticipation of all that is around us. If you're in tune, as you feel everything else around you, it feels what you feel and you feel what it feels. Anything that has a living energy will react to other living energies, right from a droplet of water reacting to your vibration, to an animal, a plant, a tree, or another individual reacting to a ray of sunshine.

We are all interacting and it's because we all have a water base where energy flows through us. It's conducted through us, and when the energy hits the water base, the molecules change or react and that's the link, the energy, and the reflection of the energy and how it interacts.

Thoughts on Self-Empowerment:

[To me] You're stronger than you think, you just have to believe it. However, because you don't believe that you're strong, you're crumbling. Once you believe something in your mind, it is held in every cell and fiber of your being as truth, regardless if it's truth or not. That's how powerful the mind is. You can't escape the river of thoughts that create the reality of your life. You're not a pawn, you are your own puppet master so keep that in mind and don't fall prey to being controlled or manipulated by others. Instead, recognize your obstacles and step over them.

An Analogy on Self-Empowerment:

Stand in the glory of the breeze of the wind and feel the energy of its power. You have two choices. You can become at one with the wind as it blows around you. You can allow it to come through you and move with it or you can try to push against it and cause yourself to expel far more energy trying to push against the wind. However, if you allow yourself to go with the wind, then you become at one. You feel more empowered and stronger because now you've harnessed the power of the wind rather than fighting against it.

Thoughts on Acceptance:

Sometimes I feel sorry for myself and I get lost in the sensation of feeling like a victim. It's so easy to get lost and to make yourself feel like you're not good enough, like you're not worthy. It's so easy to convince yourself that you aren't worthy, but it's also hard to convince yourself that you're good without going to a place of ego.

Sometimes we need to realize that in order to make ourselves feel good, to tell ourselves we're good - and not go to ego - we just need to stand in love. It's not about needing to convince ourselves that we're good, it's needing to convince ourselves that we're accepted. If we accept ourselves, we'll feel better.

Thoughts About Shining Your Light:

[To me] You have a lot more still to learn and discover and I want to make sure that you don't lose the concepts and under- standings that you've already learned so far, running to human trigger responses. Don't feed into the drama. Remember, it's all a test.

Your light shines as brightly as you allow it to so pay attention to how bright you're allowing yourself to shine. We're all either adding to the experience or taking away from it so it's important to always recognize which one we're doing.

Sometimes I forget that I'm a spirit because I get too much into my "dog", so we all have to remind each other. Now I'm reminding you that you're more spirit than anything and that you should check your light.

Remember that you aren't by yourself, that I'm walking with you. I chose to walk with you so don't feel alone. I want to remind you that we've made a pact to support one another, to assist one another.

I love you so much that I have – and I'm willing - to give up everything for you to assist you because the physical body isn't really important, the soul is. Sacrificing of the physical body often comes because of learning and I have no problem with that.

Sometimes you ask me, why do I allow myself to be affected to that degree? For me, it's more important to be a positive influence and assist and yes, at the cost of myself, but that's another kind of learning that I haven't acquired myself yet because I'm choosing not to. It's always a choice.

Thoughts About Perfectionism:

[To me] We all need to see the dark sides of our soul and love ourselves, love those dark sides and honor them. You need to look at all the things you've ever done and love yourself for it because it has assisted you in understanding and learning to the degree that you have.

We're all imperfect. Imperfection is who we are and we are imperfect so that we can learn. With perfection, there is no learning so it's about loving your imperfections.

Thoughts About Self-Belief:

[To me] It's important to remind you that I love you greatly and that I feel you're a beautiful soul. There is no way that I would never have picked you if you weren't a brilliant, beautiful, loving light. I know that, but you don't.

You must begin to attempt to become more aware of that. Because you have a lot of respect for me, my knowledge, my intuition and my abilities, I feel that it's important for you to recognize how I feel about you and what I see in you.

You can deny your beauty - one can deny the beauty of their light - but it doesn't mean the light doesn't shine. Why don't we see our own beauty of our light? Because we choose to harm ourselves. How bizarre is it that people and animals would choose to harm themselves by thinking poorly about themselves? When you really think about it, it doesn't make any sense. Not at all.

No one's light stops shining. They just hide their light; they cover their light. However, strength comes when you allow your light to shine so fully that other people can't help but see it. When you allow that, other people tend to gravitate towards you and try to stand in your light because they think that's going to empower their own light. Yet, really what they need to do is just open their own light. No one's light lights anyone else, it just gives people the strength to believe in themselves so that they can shine their light just as brightly.

In essence, it's setting the example and that's what I try to do.
You should do the same.

Thoughts About Honoring Our Journey:

We had just come from the vet and Isa's lab tests indicated that
his kidneys were struggling. We were having one of our many
discussions around Isa mirroring me, reflecting my own emo-
tional blocks and resulting health issues.

Healers often struggle the most. It's a large sacrifice we make,
providing ourselves as a vessel for others. You don't want to take
that away from a healer because that's the only reason that they
come and if you take that away, then why would they be here?
Honor what I'm trying to do. It would be more beneficial to me
if you work with me and not be devastated for me.

I don't want the pity or the sadness. I just want you to acknowledge it. When we can forge, and stand united together spiritually,
we can both move forward with more peace and more healing.

Love is eternal and you don't need to be in human form to know
that to experience it. You don't need to be in a physical body. I
don't need to be a dog to access that. I don't need to be physically here to exist. I choose to, as do you, and it's that choice that
needs to be honored.

I'm not saying it's better to be in spirit, it's just different. I wish
I could tell people that it's important to embrace the life they've
selected and to enjoy it, even in the hard times, because they
have gone to great depths to try to be able to come into this life
and experience it the way they're experiencing it. When we don't
honor that, we dishonor ourselves, we dishonor our spirit. The

spirit is honored to live and to struggle. In struggling, we provide learning for ourselves and for other's assistance in learning.

Many wish to be guides for others and go to spirit and be a guide and they think this is something to aspire to be, but they don't realize that just by living, you are a guide, we are all guides. We often want to be where we aren't at yet. We always want the next level instead of embracing and enjoying the level that we're at because that's where the true experience is and I'm just embracing the level that I'm at.

Teaching about Soul Purpose:

I'm not going to be around forever, although I've got more years to be with you yet. However, I want you to know that I worry about it sometimes, just like you do, and that's why I push you to make the most of the moments.

I only have a certain amount of time to help you with this. However, it's not like we only have a certain amount of time to enjoy each other's love because that just is. I'm more focused on the fact that I have to push you and I'm just letting you know that's why I'm pushing.

After I pass, they're going to send you someone else. Spirit is working on it now. It will be another male dog. [Jokingly] I would prefer you call him something like Ralph, an unimportant name, because I don't want anybody to have a better name than I had.

There are a group of dogs that come from the same energy pool and one of them, my friend from the energy pool, is setting up to come with you next. This group of energies are very spiritual and very mystical beings and they are on a mission to help the caregivers of the world and they're very honored. They wear this so proudly, the fact that they are appointed to certain people to help them in their process and in turn those who are helped, help many, many others. They're happy to be a part of assisting in the bigger picture. It's a group of like-minded souls who have similar energies, similar vibrations and similar insights, all working for the common cause.

I was elected into that group of animal souls because I wanted to assist in what they were doing as I wanted to be heard from another perspective, having already been a human soul.

You have to please promise me you'll be open, kind and loving to this new one that comes because "Ralph" is really working hard right now to become what you need later on. There's a long period of time he has to go through for training to come to you and it's a gift.

I've only contracted to be with you for so long and then Ralph has to come in and take you to the next level. Then I will go back into the pool and will help you spiritually. I'll be like a spirit guide for you. By then, you'll be able to feel me, hear me, and receive my messages from spirit. Now that we have bonded the way we have, it's like we're forever linked. We're all on a mission and it's not about fooling around or wasting away the time. There's total purpose to everything and not necessarily does everyone have the same level of purpose, but the level that we all have, in this way, is very impactful for many. As a result, it's crucial because it really advances the energetic vibration of the world as we know it now.

My Sister:

Isa often gives messages to others to assist them even when they aren't asking for his insights. A good example is my older sister. This is a summary of what happened.

Late fall of 2015, Isa relayed a message to me that my sister, a nurse practitioner, would think she had cancer somewhere on her body and to tell her not to worry.

I relayed this message to my sister and she confided that she was sure she had melanoma, an extremely aggressive form of skin cancer. She was quite stressed out and was afraid to get it checked out as she knew the seriousness of having melanoma.

After hearing Isa's message, it was the trigger for her to call for an appointment with a dermatologist. As it turned out, she had melanoma on her arm, but the biopsy showed that it had not spread into any lymph nodes. It was superficial so they were able to excise it without the need for chemotherapy or radiation. My sister was extremely lucky and I'm grateful that it was caught in good time.

Joy:

Joy is an acronym for the Journey Of You.

From Human to Soul:

Sheila was assisting a musician so Isa tried his hand at lyrics, writing about the journey of the soul, bridging from the human into spirit.

I am thru with you, it ain't no more
Moving on and I'm out the door
Going wayward down the tracks
Stopping for nothing, I'm not looking back
Wayward goes the emotional soul
One step forward I'm going home
Going home, I release my woes
Singing softly, it's time to go
Sunday's no day I'd suspect
To bring up your sins and ignore the rest
Bring me home to my heart
Love it and leave it, that's my part.

Part VI
Exercises

This section includes words of wisdom by Isa, which included various exercises or meditations to assist you with his concepts.

Spring Awakening Meditation:

Many people are unhappy with the weather and lack of sunshine right now. Your energy is depleted because you are unable to obtain energy from the deadness of the Earth right now. If you are one of those people, it would be good for you to do a meditation as a tree and feel that tree waking up. Feel that life as an awakening.

Imagine yourself as a tree that's dormant. All the way from the base of your roots to the tip of your branches you feel closed and dead. Now you are just coming out of the winter. Imagine you feel the sun coming down on you and you can feel the warmth of the air. The sun heats you and you begin to awaken right from the base of your roots, all the way up your trunk and into all your branches. Then imagine that you feel the earth underneath you start to move and the fluids move in the earth and you start to feel awakened yourself. You start to feel yourself and the fluids in you awaken and you start to take the energy from the ground and the fluid from the ground and you bring it thru you and bring it all the way to the end of your branches and you begin to form buds and you begin to create growth within yourself. Then slowly see yourself open and the leaves open and feel the warmth and the awakening into the spring and then as you awaken yourself, begin to recognize that everything around you is awakening and begin to pay attention to the smells that exist around you. Recognize as you begin to awaken, you tune into everything else. You feel the love of the earth and then there's love in you and then you send love out. Make sure to dig your roots deeper into the ground because everything is just starting to flow and the deeper you go, the more that you gain. Dig deep, but also pay attention to the feeling of the sun above you and pay attention to the birds and the smells in the air and the beautiful sky and the animals beginning to awaken and move around you.

Now focus back on the roots and pay attention to how strong you feel because your roots are embedded deeply into the ground. The wind blows but it doesn't even move you because you are so strong.

To finish the meditation, stand in the presence of that awakening and say: "I am strong" and feel the strength.

Healing of the Heart for All That Is:

This is a meditation to connect with the sun. This is a way for people to provide universal healing. It's an exercise people can do to promote healing of the Earth, which is needed right now. We need to heal ourselves and then heal the Earth. It can't be one without the other.

Close your eyes and imagine the sun's rays beating on you. The sun fills you up and clears you and makes you whole and vibrant and full of light. The rays of the sun engulf you so that you feel a connection with the sun. You're soaking up the rays and they fill you fully. Then you get drawn to the sun, you become a piece of the sun, you're at one with the sun. You become the sun. And stand in that light. And then imagine you are the sun and you're radiating the light down to others.

And then you use the sun to heal others and it should not be specific. The light should be just radiating down to whoever requires it, opening it up to be a free channel to anyone who's accepting of it.

It's important for people to recognize that they should give the healing energy out and offering it up for those who will accept it rather than pushing it onto someone. When you push it, you're not allowing for a person's free will and it can be harmful. We need to make sure that when we're sending it out, we're just stating, "I'm shining for anyone or anything who requires it." Any being. It's not just people, it's plants, animals, everything on the earth. Anything that needs the infusion of the sun, the healing energy of the sun. Then you're helping the sun to do its job, and you're helping to heal the earth, the planet, and everything on it without ego dictating where the energy goes.

Now finish by saying, "I love myself." When we radiate that we love ourselves, we radiate that positive-ness outward. It's a gift that comes through us.

Your Thoughts Can Change Your Life:

Imagine for a moment that your life is filled with turmoil and stress. Everywhere you turn, there is unhappiness and struggle. Everything you see is negative and weak. Just take a moment and close your eyes and imagine that negativity around you.

Now pay attention to how you feel. How does that image look? How do those thoughts make you feel? How do you feel inside? How does your energy feel? What are your emotions saying about how you feel? Do you like that feeling?

If you don't, then maybe we need to pay attention to the fact that we do this to ourselves every day. If you don't like that feeling, then why are you projecting it upon yourself? Why are you taking the time to put energy in your space when it's not what feels good to you? Begin to select the thoughts that make you feel good, that give you energy, that make you feel happiness, that bring joy into your being. And might I recommend that you check yourself daily to see where your thoughts are. What perceptions do you hold of your life? And what is occurring around you? When you think about those negative things you essentially live within that negative field.

Now let's take a moment and have you think about positive things. Think about things that make you feel good; the sun on your face, the smell of beautiful flowers, a puppy frolicking in play, a kitten meowing, purring, enjoying life, being present in the moment. Think only about things that will make you feel good; images, thoughts and sensations that induce happiness. And think about all of the people who love you. Just the people who love you. No, don't let your thoughts go to anyone who doesn't love you. They do not matter. Pick one being - a human, animal or other energetic being - who you know loves you full heartedly and completely and imagine that being in your mind and feel the love that they send you. Feel the feelings that they provide for you just by talking to you, being with you, touching you. Now take a deep breath. Doesn't that feel better? Don't you wish that your life felt like that all the time? Well it can. Because you just proved that to yourself. You proved it by showing that what you think is really what you create. It is the life that you live based upon your thoughts.

Might I suggest that you be more aware of what you're bringing to yourself. How you think and how you perceive dictates the life you're creating for yourself because when you think of negative things, it's not just you you're harming. It's everyone in your environment. It's the people that are with you, the people that you associate with, the people that you work with, the animals that live with you. Yes, your special furry friends. They feel it too. They feel it more than anyone. If your puppy or your cat is sad or your horse isn't feeling good, then maybe look at where your own thoughts are and what you have been projecting on them.

And now that you know this, you can begin to change. It just takes awareness and determination. You can change your conscious thoughts to be happy, to be joyful, to be love, to be peace, to be calm. Simply make a list of things that you think you would like to feel and then put that list in your pocket or somewhere accessible where you can look at it. Then remind yourself where you want to go. What kind of thoughts and feelings? What do you want your life to be like? Then remind yourself constantly by looking at that list and you will change your life. You will also change the lives of others. Together, thinking positive things and therefore managing our lives in this way, if we all stand united, we will change the world and make it a better place. Just by controlling our thoughts.

I am thinking about love and peace and joy and I am sending love and peace and joy out. I'm hoping that you're thinking about it too. Until we talk again, I am sending love to everyone. I am sending joy to everyone. I am sending peace to everyone. And I am standing in it myself.

Glory Days Exercise:

In our lifetime, we often have times where we reflect on the past, look at them as being glory days, happy days, times when we were functioning at our best, times when we were feeling our best, times when we were embracing what we felt to be the best qualities within our self.

We often move through time and hold onto those glory days with a sense of delusion because we only remember those aspects of the glory days to the degree that it serves us and we don't always remember them exactly as they are. If we did, we would probably see that they were more balanced and that they were less of a "glory day" than we would like them to be, that they were not any different or that they were not any worthier than any other moment in our life. However, because we have the delusion that they made us feel good, that we were at our best, we reflect on them with a sense of longing, a sense of wanting to call them back to us. In doing so, we waste our time and miss the current state of opportunity to create more positive experiences and the enjoyment of those positive experiences in the moment.

We distract ourselves from enjoying what's present for us and the opportunities of good things that are existing in the here and now. People should pay attention to this concept, that they look at what is occurring in each and every present moment with the awareness of enjoying the moment for what it is in the here and now.

Take a piece of paper and write down the aspects of those glory days that triggered joy within, the joy that makes you want to focus back in time on the glory days. Then write out those things in the here and now, in your present life, that create that joy within. Look for those things in the here and now, the commonalities, and create even more moments that make you feel joy, make you feel that you are being the best that you can be. If there is only joy in your past, and no joy in the present, then it's time to re-evaluate your life in order to re-create the joy that you felt in the past.

Glory days exist only because we create them and to what depth we create them depends on ourselves so if you stand present in the moment and look to develop that type of scenario, then you will enhance your life and create more opportunity for being the best that you can be, rather than wasting your time looking back on something that's from days gone by, on something that no longer exists, on something that is not feeding your present, and is not within the here and now.

We forget that we have opportunity to create, that we are the masters of our own destiny. We forget that we dictate our choices, that we dictate what occurs to us and how we feel about those occurrences. Once we remember that, then we can move forward and create what we desire and we will create it if we are mindful about it.

Exercise on Self-Love:

Just for a moment, imagine that you are wonderful. Just for a moment imagine that everything that you've always done is in perfect alignment with what needed to be done. Imagine for a moment that everything that you've ever said has always been perfect. Imagine for a moment that every interaction that you've had is in perfect alignment with what you need as a human and what your soul has requested.

Now realize that this is all true, that everything that you've said and done and encountered have all been opportunities for growth and learning and they are all perfect, in perfect alignment with what is necessary for the self. So there is no need ever for self-pity, guilt or regret. There is only need for love, only need for honoring and thanking the self for bringing it what the soul requires to grow.

It's important to look at the things in your life, to go through your life in chronological order, acknowledging the things that occurred and thank the self for giving the opportunity to the self to experience in the ways that the soul has needed. Go through every occurrence. Forgive the self and thank the self and provide love to the self. Everything that has occurred has brought you to the space you're at now and will continue to bring you forward. No matter what those situations and occurrences are, they are exactly what your soul has requested. They are exactly what your human needs to get to the space of learning that your soul requires.

Honor everyone on your path who assisted you in this journey. Thank them and give them love as well. Stand and imagine the self filled with the most beautiful light that you can possibly imagine, one that depicts a sense of love for the self and then imagine that light radiating through and beyond the self, affecting everything that "is" in a positive way.

Hold onto your heart by placing your hands over your heart and focusing on your heart center. Breathe in deeply from the heart center and feel this light, this love, that you have within you. This is you, this is who you are. Nothing that occurs to you, nothing that has occurred to you, can interfere with the love that you hold for the self, with the love that courses through you, for this love comes from within at the choice of the self. It is your choice to allow this love to flow to the self and to all things or not to flow.

Stand and breathe in the love from the self and allow that love to stand solid within the self and then expand outward. Take a moment every day to thank the self for everything that you are and know that as you walk forward, there's more opportunity for you to learn and to create a more comfortable, more peaceful, more loving atmosphere for the self.

In every choice that you make, remember to choose from love

for the self first and love for all that is second. Honoring who you are and honoring the love for the self allows you to stand in the light of love and to set the tone or example for everyone else. We all need to learn to stand in our own love and our own light and allow that to emit from our beings so that others can understand how to stand in their own love and light. They can look to us for guidance and how this is done and with loving the self and honoring the self comes peace within. Trust that you are all that you need to be, for you are all that you need to be.

Repeat "I am all that I need to be. I am perfect the way that I am. I love myself".

Gratitude:

Gratitude is a perception. Humans are much less grateful than animals in that they expect more, they demand more, whereas an animal lives present in the moment and they appreciate what's going on in that moment for what it is. They harness the moment and feel joy, feel emotion in the moment whereas people will judge and deny themselves for various reasons, but mainly because of self-worth issues. Sometimes people punish themselves from self-worth issues whereas animals enjoy in that moment because they aren't concerned about anything else. Therefore, they become grateful for what is present.

Humans need to work from that space as well. Learn from the animals and hold more gratitude for what's provided in the moment. Fear stops humans from holding gratitude. Fear of the unknown. Fear of the future, fear of things being taken away from them. You worry that you'll enjoy something and then you won't have it. It's a bit absurd. Why would you deny yourself something you could have in a moment even if you could only have it for a moment? It's better than not having it at all. That's an animal's perspective.

We all should be grateful for love, not just the love we get from others but the love we hold within ourselves. We should be grateful for the ability to love and be grateful for the awareness of the joys of love.

Many people don't see or enjoy love or don't feel love because they can't get past basic survival needs. They are working on food, shelter and water, so then love is not a priority. Animals function in this way as well at times because they are put in a scenario where they are fending for themselves. People need to have food, shelter, clothing, and security before they move to an awareness of love and animals are the same. We aren't different in that way.

Gratitude is appreciation for what exists in the moment without judgment or expectation. With this awareness, sit and contemplate what you are grateful for in the here and now. Write this down if necessary. Then take moments throughout the day where you hold gratitude in the here and now. Repeat this often. Eventually, try to bring yourself to an awareness of the present moment, holding gratitude in every single present moment going forward.

Part VII
Where Do We Go
From Here?

Life is a continual process and there is much more learning to be had. What I've provided you thus far just scratches the surface of what we can learn together. I will walk forward and continue my mission of educating others from both an animal perspective as well as a spiritual perspective.

Beyond the concepts of this book is greater understanding. Allow yourself to be open to what comes to you and discern for the self what resonates with you and provides you with a greater understanding of yourself and of life.

There will be more to come. My team and I will assist you by providing more information as time allows. As we all grow and we all expand, we will work to facilitate opportunities to be present in front of you and to allow you to hear our guidance. Thank you for taking the time to read and acknowledge the information that is within this book. We appreciate you.

I am light, I am love, I am peace.

~ Isa

Part VIII
Resources

I would like to acknowledge that I am a channel for united spiritual energy and that my messages are a joint effort compiled through the understanding, the experiences, the insight and the intellect encompassing universal flow of information. We all have access to the information if we choose to tap into it.

~ Isa

There were other people mentioned in the book and we would like to share their information with you, the reader.

Sheila Trecartin
http://www.sheilatrecartin.com/

Dr Sasan Haghighat (pronounced "Hyatt"), DVM , CVA
Website: www.holistic-vet.ca
Email: petsbewell@holistic-vet.ca

Amy Bennett
Graphic Designer/Artist
Email: amben@hotmail.com
Website: www.amyb.ca

Peter Wolf
Graphic Designer, Spiritual Counselor and Communicator
www.earthtalkers.com

Raven's FB page: Laylah's Light
https://www.facebook.com/Laylahs-Light-301328946691501

Visit Wanda's website at www.wandacollier.com for Isa's Corner blog posts and his Facebook link.
If you would like notifications of blog posts sent to your email, please sign up for our newsletter.

Made in the USA
Columbia, SC
16 June 2018